Sibylle Princess of Prussia
Frederick William Prince of Prussia

**The King's Love**
Frederick the Great
His Gentle Dogs and Other Passions

Sibylle Princess of Prussia
Frederick William Prince of Prussia

# The King's Love

Frederick the Great
*His Gentle Dogs and Other Passions*

Translated from the German
by Dennis McCort

Palm**Art**Press
Berlin

## Photo Credits

Archiv für Kunst und Geschichte: 18, 42, 80, 91; Haus Preußen: 35, 110; Porzellanmanufaktur Meißen: 129; Schloss Bayreuth – Bayerische Verwaltung der staatlichen Schlösser, Gärten und Seen: 31, 66; Stiftung Preußische Schlösser und Gärten Berlin-Brandenburg (SPSG): 10, 14, 24, 50, 67, 71, 75, 76, 82, 113, 136, 153, 159; Stiftung Preußischer Kulturbeseitz, Geheimes Staatsarchiv: 60, 157; Staatliche Museen zu Berlin, Kupferstichkabinett: 104.

The remaining illustrations derive from the following volumes:
Franz Kugler, Geschichte Friedrichs des Großen, Leipzig 1856: 98, 142, 147; Paul Seidel, Friedrich der Große und die bildenden Kunst Leipzig/Berlin 1922, S. 162: 47; Gustav Berthold Volz (Hg.), Friedrich der Große im Spiegel seiner Zeit, Bd. 3, Berlin 1926/27, S. 41: 56.

Bibliografische Information der Deutschen Nationalbibliothek
Die Deutsche Nationalbibliothek verzeichnet diese Publikation in der Deutschen Nationalbibliografie; detaillierte bibliografische Daten sind im Internet über http://www.dnb.de abrufbar.

ISBN: 978-3-96258-047-6

English Edition, 2020 © PalmArtPress, Berlin
German Edition: © Sibylle Prinzessin von Preußen
1 - 3. Auflage, Siedler Verlag, München, in der Verlagsgruppe Random House GmbH

PalmArtPress
Pfalzburger Str. 69, 10719 Berlin
Publisher: Catharine J. Nicely
www.palmartpress.com

Cover photo: *Friedrich der Große in Rheinsberg*, Fedor Poppe
English translation: Dennis McCort
Layout: Nicely Media, Julia Koschitzki
Print: Schaltungsdienst Lange, Berlin

Printed in Germany

# Content

# I
## Prolog

*You'll find it odd that an old man like me could lose
his heart to a little dog. For fourteen years Thisbe
was my constant companion; she was loyal to me
like that queen of Babylon whose name I gave her.
Perhaps she was enchanted! On many an occasion
I believed it! Whenever I couldn't sleep at night, she
would lie next to me and look at me quite curiously
– like a good soul!*[1]

The female Italian greyhound being mourned by
Frederick the Great had died that afternoon. The King
himself was already seventy-one years old, and his
close relationship to these sensitive little dogs had en-
dured over decades. In 1744, almost forty years earlier,
his first pet she-dog *Biche* had been allowed to accompany him to the spa at Bad Pyrmont and, a month later,
to the Second Silesian War.

For Frederick friendship and love were always of
existential importance, but they were also a source of
great suffering. The loss of those closest to him caused
him profound suffering. As his private correspondence
shows, he had great difficulty overcoming experiences
involving death or separation. With increasing age the
King, growing lonely and intolerant of human weakness, came to prefer the company of his dainty dogs.
All his life Frederick nurtured great sympathy for
animals. Consequently, as an equestrian he made use

of neither whips nor spurs. Once called out on this by an astonished valet, he is said to have challenged the man to bare his stomach and allow a sharp object to be plunged into it. He gave his horses euphonious names such as Cerberus, Tiger and Sternrapp (Star Steed). As king he also named them after statesmen and military leaders such as Pitt, Kaunitz, Brühl and Condé and fed them luscious fruits. When Catherine the Great wanted to make him, as ruler of Prussia, the gift of an Arabian dromedary, he accepted it only after an expert report had confirmed that the animal could tolerate the Mark's climate. And upon the death of one of the Rheinsberg palace monkeys of consumption, he was moved to have the rest of them returned to their warm native habitat. The King's affection for his Italian greyhounds was, of course, especially intense, having its origins as it did in his deep and tender friendships with human beings. It was the extraordinary Count Frederick Rudolph of Rothenburg who presented him with the she-dog *Biche*. And it was the former's death that led the King to issue that renowned private testament of 11 January 1752, in which he decreed that he did not wish to be laid to rest in a sarcophagus beside his family members, this in accord with the burial ceremonial of the day, but rather in a more modest grave, with his dogs, who in life had been permitted to share his bed with him. By the time he issued this testamentary directive shortly before his 40th birthday, he had already lived through wars, lost intimates and just barely escaped execution himself.

## II
### *Keeps His Hair like a Fool's*
### The Sensitive Crown Prince
### (1712-1729)

Frederick's life was rife with great drama; again and again he had to overcome harrowing experiences that pushed him to the brink of despair and significantly compromised his health. Nevertheless, he was, to the end of his life, an unusually strong ruler, who, as Goethe characterized him in his *elegy, still stood where others wavered,* and upon whom, as the victor in the Second Silesian War, the populace of Berlin bestowed the honorific epithet *the Great.*

An essential factor in Frederick's extreme personality structure was doubtless the contradictory characters of his parents, who made him the apple of their eye from childhood on, the father ultimately having – in the truest sense of the word – the more dominant influence. Just like Frederick's grandfather, the first Prussian king, his father Frederick William I had married a princess who was far superior to him in terms of ancestry and cultural breeding. Both the grandmother of Frederick the Great, Queen Sophie Charlotte, and his mother, Sophie Dorothea, came from Guelphic houses oriented to French culture and to the splendor of the Sun King of Versailles. Along with the Bourbons, the Guelphs were among the most distinguished noble families on the continent. Sophie Dorothea's father had been, as Elector of Hanover, and, in addition, as George I,

Frederick William I wanted to base Prussia's power on a strong army. From 1725 on the *Soldier King* always wore a uniform in public, here a decorative cuirass in the painting by Antoine Pesne (ca. 1733).

King of England since 1714. Both queens were accustomed to being surrounded by the glitterati of society and conversant with the most prominent artists and scholars of their time. They strove to establish this cultural niveau in backward Brandenburg-Prussia as well – the grandmother with greater, the mother with less, success.

On January 18, 1701, in Königsberg, Frederick's grandfather, the Elector of Brandenburg, placed the crown of Frederick I, the first King in Prussia, on his own head. In order to do justice to the grandeur of the occasion, no less to the Queen's high demands, he approved enormous sums of money for grand displays of splendor, the backlash of which would be felt by his son Frederick William I on his ascension to the throne in 1713. He was forced to take over a state mired deeply in debt. He reduced the royal household to a minimum, sold unnecessary coaches, jewels and diamonds, and set an example with his own life of what he demanded of his subjects: frugality, discipline and rigor for the welfare of the state. He thereby took a totally different path from nearly all other rulers of his time.

Frederick William I, however, expected compliance with his strict guidelines not only from his subjects but from his closest family members as well. This lifestyle was hard to bear for his consort Sophie Dorothea; she loved French art and literature and created her own little cultured world in Monbijou Palace, with library, porcelain and art collections. The Frederick biographer Reinhold Koser wrote about this at the end of the nineteenth century in a tone astonishingly caustic for the Wilhelmine period: *From her the children inherited, amidst the philistine prose with which they grew up, a rich dowry of ideas, a joy in the pleasing surface of things, a more refined taste, an eye for what was beautiful, a vein for literature.* [2]

The first child of this most dissimilar royal couple, born to them in 1707, was at once the expected heir to the throne. All rejoicing over the event turned to grief, however, when the boy died a few months after his birth. On the 3rd of July, 1709, a princess was born, Wilhelmine, who, alas, evoked only modest joy and was, as she herself remarked in retrospect, *received quite ungraciously since everyone passionately wanted a prince.*[3]

The following year Sophie Dorothea finally gave birth to another boy, who in the summer of 1711 likewise died. A fourth pregnancy led, on Sunday, January 24, 1712, to the birth of a third heir apparent; yet the newborn was of such delicate constitution that once again the court was compelled to fear for his life. But little Crown Prince Frederick flourished, even if as a frail and, by all accounts, difficult child.

A deep emotional bond formed between him and his sister Wilhelmine, a bond no doubt strengthened by the fact that, as the oldest of a total of ten siblings, they grew up together in their first years and even as children joined forces against their tyrannical father. *Never have brother and sister loved each other so tenderly,* wrote Wilhelmine of this deep friendship in her memoirs.[4]

In the summer of 1714 when Frederick was two and a half years old and his sister just five, Queen Sophie Dorothea commissioned the French painter Antoine Pesne, whom she held in high regard, to do the first double portrait of the two children. Even in this early painting Frederick is shown with a little dog, which in itself is nothing unusual. The Queen loved lapdogs and had, among others, a little Bolognese, with which she posed for a portrait herself years later. Moreover, the little toy dog was frequently used as a companion to the royal child in portraits. This genre of child portraiture harked back to the painting of the 16th century, above all to Titian, and was very much in fashion until well into the 18th century. As a rule, the children were depicted with a cute, long-haired toy spaniel or a Bolognese: thus Frederick's prematurely deceased oldest brother, the little Prince Frederick Louis of Prussia, in a posthumous painting also by Antoine Pesne. For contrast in the double portrait, Pesne placed a small hunting dog at young Frederick's side, which, taken together with the similarly depicted side drum, was perhaps intended to emphasize rather the manly side of the heir to the throne. For the – as his father disparagingly called him – *effeminate* lad took greater pleasure in his sister's games than in the hunt or the military. Yet the scenario does not seem to have been mounted explicitly for the painting. The picture's year of origin, 1714, was also the year of Frederick Wilhelm I's imminent campaign against Charles XII of Sweden, who had

*Heaven gave us the same sensitivity,* Frederick wrote to his favorite sister at age forty; from earliest childhood she was the most important woman in his life. The painting by Antoine Pesne of 1714 shows Frederick as Crown Prince with his sister Wilhelmine.

laid siege to Stralsund. According to one anecdote, it was gripping stories like the one about the occupation of Stettin by 24,000 Russians that Frederick heard in his father's milieu and that inspired his drumming.

While Wilhelmine, as usual, wanted them to wreathe flowers together and play with dolls, to the surprise of everyone the Crown Prince all at once began beating the drum in march step. He is even said to have energetically lectured his sister: *Drumming is more useful to me than playing and preferable to flowers.* [5] This little story appears to have a kernel of truth. There are at least two passages in the letters of Queen Sophie Dorothea to her husband indicating that the Crown Prince's newly awakened military proclivities could have influenced the genesis of the picture. On July 15, 1714, she writes, *Fritz says that he would like to learn his drill steps, to please you when you return,* and in a letter two days later she tells her husband, *I've had the children painted and believe their portraits are coming out well.*[6] On close inspection, the painting actually offers no military scenery, drum, hunting dog and soldier notwithstanding. The soldier standing guard is set apart at the left margin, brother and sister forming the center of the composition. Behind Wilhelmine a black attendant carries a parasol and a parrot. Frederick, bedecked with the Order of the Black Eagle and a sash, is girded with a drum; the drumstick in his right hand points in the distance, thereby becoming a toy, a twig, for the little dog as it turns its head towards it in an attitude of readiness for play. The stick in his left hand, which his sister covers with her right, lies across the drum. And while Frederick looks up to Wilhelmine, she gazes with serious mien in the direction of the observer.

The result is that Pesne has created an interesting double portrait of the siblings, one that, first and foremost, does not, as past interpretations frequently had it, *show the great King pressing for warlike deeds even as a small child.* The picture anticipates rather an entirely pacifist passion of the Crown Prince, his love for playful, untrained little dogs. It was not for their aptitude for hunting (which Frederick abhorred, as he was later to declare among other things in letters to his sister and in his *Antimachiavell*), but rather their sensitive, subservient nature, their guilelessness and loyalty, that Italian greyhounds became his constant companions. He thereby settled on a breed of dog that was not considered especially select at that time. In the eighteenth century owning Italian greyhounds was – in contrast to owning traditional hunting dogs – not exclusively the prerogative of the upper classes; ordinary citizens too possessed these dogs, such as the brewer Kahlbaum of New Market Square in Potsdam. Italian greyhounds, a dwarf form of the greyhound, are extremely capricious creatures of petite stature, which, with a shoulder height of thirty-five centimeters, weigh scarcely more than four kilograms. They react to external stimuli with excessive sensitivity, their trembling observable even in sunshine. For this reason the King is said to have pressed these delicate creatures to his breast under his vest on excursions, which possibly even pleased the animals, since, as a rule, the little creatures seek the immediate proximity of their caregivers. The French writer Alphonse Lamartine (1790–1869), who like Frederick rejected treatment of his sick dogs by reputedly incompetent doctors, attests: *To this day, physicians have not recognized that the Italian greyhound is not a dog but rather a four-legged bird ...* a bird, moreover, that commands an extraordinarily fine intuitive sense. Irritable moods and dissemblance are almost unbearable to them. Anyone whom Frederick's dogs liked was regarded by him as well with greater favor. If he happened to be in a bad temper, the dogs exerted themselves to cheer him up, by bringing him little leather balls which he had ordered to be made for them and which lay everywhere throughout the palace. Apart from their situational hyperarousal, the King's gentle companions were extremely tranquil animals. The personal physician Zimmermann remarked following a visit to Sanssouci, *They never stir and never made a sound in my presence.* They just sat quietly on the sofas close to their master or lay in his lap or at his feet, as he wrote.

It was not until adulthood that Frederick discovered his fondness for Italian greyhounds. As a child his love went unconditionally to Wilhelmine, who was his friend and role model. He was guided by the preferences of his older sister, who enjoyed spending her time on little theater pieces, costumes, dolls and flowers. As opposed to his father, his mother had no objection to these pastimes. Queen Sophie Dorothea rejected her husband's sternness, thrift and philistinism. Conflict was inevitable. *If the King learned*

Sophie Dorothea shared her love of small dogs with her six daughters, who upon the Queen's death preserved the numerous portraits of her dogs. (Antoine Pesne, 1737)

*that the Prince was putting on his sister's clothes and was playing with her in French comedies under the mother's supervision, or that he was reading books unsuitable for him, then acrimony and punishment were the sure result. Coddled by his mother, harshly disciplined by his father, the boy grew ... into a youth.* [7]

But, to the great chagrin of his sister, he also developed his own interests. At age nine the Crown Prince developed a passion for adventure novels, among which Fénelon's *Les Aventures de Télémaque* with its idealized image of a wise monarchy made the deepest impression on him. He now found himself unable to share Wilhelmine's predilection for little lapdogs any longer. Queen Sophie Dorothea and Wilhelmine spoiled their pugs, Bolog-neses and dwarf spaniels beyond all measure, which even the King looked upon with favor. Thus did Johann Christian Lieberkühn, court goldsmith to Frederick William I – astonishingly, the *Soldier King* had a pen-chant for ostentatious silver – , craft in 1720 at the Queen's behest *2 pairs of earrings for a tiny little dog.*[8] Invoices from the years 1724-25 document that Sophie Dorothea also had portraits painted of her little dears many times over and even had one of her little lapdogs that had died in spring 1725 stuffed.[9] In her memoirs Wilhelmine relates a little episode in which the dogs also play a part, even though the main sub-ject is the permanent conflict between children and father. In 1726 the Queen took pains to divert the at-tention of the stern Frederick William I from a small chest containing compromising letters written by the brothers and sisters, letters in which the latter had ex-pressed criticism of their father; this she did by asking her husband to arbitrate an issue concerning the dogs present at the scene: *She [the Queen] had a very beauti-ful little Bolognese dog, as did I [Wilhelmine], and both dogs happened to be in the room. 'My daughter maintains her dog is more beautiful then mine,' she said to the King, 'And I prefer my own. Would you please settle the matter?' He laughed and asked me whether I loved my dog a great deal. 'With all my heart,' I said, 'after all, he's so good and clever'; my answer delighted him, he hugged me several times ... meanwhile the King was reconciled with my brother, who followed us to Potsdam.*[10]

This familial harmony did not last long. Over the years the Crown Prince's relationship to his father had plainly deteriorated, this despite the efforts of a succession of tutors and teachers on behalf of the moral development of the heir apparent. Withal the King was deeply troubled over the upbringing of the headstrong boy. When Frederick reached the age of thirteen, he took him to Potsdam under his direct supervision and appointed him captain in his own royal guard. But Frederick William's hope of exorcizing all his son's extremist tendencies through regimented intercourse with soldiers and religious education was disappointed again and again – accompanied by increasing bouts of rage. His tolerance towards his firstborn son declined even further due to the fact that there was as of 1722 an extremely obedient second son and as of 1726 a third.

The headmaster of the Graues Kloster gymnasium in Berlin, Anton Friederich Büsching, an astute observer of current events, noted: *And so he adopted the view of the Crown Prince that he was not a suitable successor to the throne, and much preferred his second* son, Prince August William, to him, since the latter was so much at home in the family circle, and just generally was at pains to please his father in all matters.[11] This climate of growing paternal disfavor became more and more intolerable to the Crown Prince. Once, after yet another reprimand from his father, the by-now sixteen-year-old son, having in early 1728 acquainted himself with the Dresden court of August the Strong with its lavish and erotic lifestyle, in contrast to the austere atmosphere in Berlin, wrote:

*Wusterhausen, September 11, 1728*
*My dear Papa!*
*I have for quite some time now not cared to venture an approach to my dear Papa, partly because it seemed to me inadvisable, mainly, however, because I anticipated a worse reception then the common one; also, out of fear of further antagonizing my dear Papa with my requests, I decided I would rather do it in writing. And so I appeal to my dear Papa for benevolence, and in so doing I can assure him that, after long reflection, my conscience makes not the slightest accusation against me for which I would have to reproach myself. However, if I should have inadvertently done something to antagonize my dear Papa, I ask for forgiveness and hope that my dear Papa will let go of the terrible hatred that I have often enough been in a position to witness in all his doings. Otherwise I would not be able to come to terms with it, since I have always believed my father to*

*be a gracious one. I trust that my dear Papa will reflect on this and once again be gracious to me.* [12]

Dear Papa promptly responds: *[You're a] willful, angry hardhead, who does not love his father; for when you love your father, you act according to his will, not only when you support it, but even when you don't see the whole picture. For another thing, you know very well that I cannot abide an effeminate lad, a lad without manly qualities, who cannot ride or shoot, and who is unclean of body as well, keeps his hair like a fool's and never trims it, and I reprimand him a thousand times for all this, but all in vain and there's no improvement in anything. And who, besides this, is arrogant, proud as a peacock, speaking to no one, neither popular nor affable, and who makes grimaces with his face, as if he were a fool, and does my will in nothing, as though restrained by force; nothing done out of love, no enthusiasm for anything but following his own whims, all else being worthless. This is my answer.*

*Frederick William.* [13]

Thus Frederick learned to hide his opinions and feelings. He lied, suppressed his tears and furtively pursued his own interests. Instead of singing church songs at the organ, he played the flute, not to mention the revolutionary game, chess, in which the pawns, and not the king and queen, are the primary captains of war; he favored chess over the board game toccadille with its red and black stones of equal value. He danced with guests at his mother's palace and had courtier's garments made for himself, among them a dressing gown of gold brocade, which he would put on after taking off his uniform, or, as he put it, his *death coat*. He went into debt for the construction of his secret library, which was housed in the residence of the fiscal councilor Julius von Pehnen and already contained several hundred volumes. Above all he loved French books, which he read mostly at night. This stressful double life, however, was not without its consequences for him. He was gaunt and effete, and frequently got sick.

At this time the court painter Antoine Pesne was again commissioned to do a portrait of the Crown Prince, now almost seventeen years old. By now Frederick had acquired a certain charisma, which his father despised but others esteemed. The admirer and biographer of Frederick, Franz Kugler, wrote, *His exterior had developed its own individual elegance; he had grown trim, his face of noble, regular formation.*[14] And Wilhelmine enthused, *He was the most charming prince one could imagine, handsome and upright, with a mind evolved far beyond his years; and he was blessed with all the gifts that distinguish an exemplary prince.*[15] Pesne rendered this charm, this *Soldier King* deflating sensibility, of the Crown Prince so subtly that it is impossible to ignore, even given the uniform of the King's regiment with its *Order of the Black Eagle*. With an open yet pensive gaze that conceals what is within, Frederick looks in the direction of the viewer. His facial expression and the placement of his hands are soft and relaxed. His right hand lies casually on his hip,

The Crown Prince, shown here in the uniform of the King's regiment with the Order of the Black Eagle, was already signing letters to Wilhelmine with *Frederick the philosopher*. A year earlier (1728), upon his first visit to the Dresden court, his flute-playing with members of the Saxon court chapel had met with great approval. Painting by Antoine Pesne from 1729.

while the half-open left hand with its outstretched index finger points down and to the left. To his right, sitting on a block of stone, is the helmet of a knight's armor – almost decorative, with no direct reference to the portrait's subject.

# III

*The King Has Utterly Forgotten That I Am His Son*
Dramatic Lessons
(1729-1740)

Frederick William I was, at this point, fully convinced that his eldest son was not suited to follow him on the throne in the future. The nine-year-old Prince August William now became the bearer of hope. Nevertheless, on the grounds of house law, the irrevocably valid right of primogeniture in the so-called male lineage, Frederick could not be passed over. As Ober-ministerialrat Büsching noted: *And so from time to time, when he was angry with him, the King would press the Crown Prince to relinquish the line of succession and yield it to his brother who was next in line … The Crown Prince, however, declared that he would rather have his head hacked off than obey the King in his unlawful demand.*[16] Frederick William I had no choice; he had to accept Frederick as legitimate heir to the throne and, moreover, prepare him for his future office. Attempts to provide sound breeding continued unabated. When the Prince came of age on his seventeenth birthday, on January 24, 1729, his teachers up to that point – Jacques Égide Duhan de Jandun, Field Marshall Albrecht Conrad Count von Finckenstein and Colonel Christoph William von Kalckstein – were replaced by Lieutenant Dietrich von Keyserlingk and Colonel Frederick William von Rochow. This was a kind of last-ditch effort, underscored by the royal directive:

*The Prince has no interest in matters of substance, he thinks only of idle pursuits, he doesn't care about his body, he has an arrogant attitude with nothing to back it up; the colonel should do everything he can to make an honest fellow and a decent officer out of him. If it doesn't work out even then, one would have to lament it before God as a calamity.*[17]

Frederick was not especially concerned about this change in personnel. *My brother liked them both well enough,* the older sister attested in her memoirs, *but Keyserlingk, as the younger and more exuberant one, was consequently more to his liking.*[18] The Crown Prince received encouragement and support behind the King's back from various quarters, and so continued to find ways to lead his life on his own terms. With respect to his private library in the fiscal councilor's house alone, he was able to increase its holdings by 3,500 volumes by the year 1730. The library encompassed an English encyclopedia, diverse dictionaries, grammars of the French, English, Italian and Spanish languages, a French rhyming lexicon, collections of anecdotes, textbooks on poetics, conversation and composition, ancient writers in French translation, historical literature, memoires, travel accounts, a survey of Brandenburg history, atlases and works of famous French writers from Rabelais to Voltaire's most recent publications – to name just a few of the books catalogued by the Prince's own hand.

The King finally realized that his efforts to mold his son had failed. His rage increased correspondingly: *[H]e couldn't lay eyes on my brother without threatening him with the cudgel*, Wilhelmine, all the while in deep concern for Frederick, was forced to conclude. *Every day he would tell me that he would put up with anything from the King, with the exception of being beaten by him; and that he, should it ever come to this extremity, would remove himself from such treatment through flight.*[19]

It did come to this *extremity*. Whereupon, in a secretly forwarded letter, the Crown Prince wrote to his mother: *I am in the deepest despair. The thing I always feared has finally happened to me. What I mean is, the King has completely forgotten that I am his son and has treated me like the lowest of all men. This morning I walked into his room as usual. Scarcely did he see me when he grabbed me by the collar and began pummeling me with his cudgel in the most horrible manner. I tried to defend myself – in vain; he was in such a terrible fury that he lost all control, and only stopped when his arm went lame from exhaustion. I have too much self-respect to put up with such treatment and have decided to put an end to it, one way or another.*[20]

Father and son were now locked in a relationship of open hatred. Frederick's sole focus was on the possibility of ending this *dog's life*, as he himself called it. He asked his confidant, the young lieutenant Hans Hermann von Katte, for support and made up his mind to flee to England, where his mother's brother reigned as King George II. The tragic outcome of the story is well known: The flight plans were revealed; Frederick Wilhelm I had the Crown Prince and von

Katte arrested in early August 1730. Wilhelmine, as a presumptive co-conspirator, was detained in the Berlin palace. For weeks she lived in anxiety over her brother, who meanwhile had been incarcerated as a prisoner of the state in the fortress at Küstrin.

A royal investigative commission was now formed to examine the motives for the Crown Prince's flight, this with the help of a questionnaire containing 185 items. In due course the matter of the succession to the throne was again brought up, the idea being that, by relinquishing his successional rights to the second eldest brother August William, Frederick might save his own life, now acutely jeopardized by his desertion. As of October 25, 1730, the military court convened in Köpenick palace. After three days the court declared itself incompetent to pass judgment on the fate of the Crown Prince *as the King's son,* since *the matter was one of state and family between a great King and his son*; the court did, however, commend the son most ardently to the father's mercy. Frederick William I was beside himself with rage over this leniency. Moreover, he had to endure the fact that his son enjoyed great sympathy within his own family and in the army, as well as among the courts of Europe. Sweden, Denmark, Holland and Russia had their envoys deliver appeals for clemency; even the Holy Roman Emperor in Vienna supported the cause of pardon. Thus Frederick's life was saved; Hans Hermann von Katte, however, was condemned to death by the King's express order.

The father declared that the Crown Prince was to observe his friend's execution in direct proximity to it.

To begin with, on the morning of November 6, 1730, the execution site at Küstrin was cordoned off by military command; then Hans Hermann von Katte walked past Frederick's barred window on the way to his execution. *Katte, forgive me. I am the cause of your death,* the Crown Prince cried out in total despair. [21] When Katte was finally executed right before his eyes, Frederick collapsed. His sister Wilhelmine reported: *The gentlemen were compelled to carry him to his bed. He lay there unconscious for several hours. When he came to, the first thing he saw was poor Katte's bloody body, which had been laid out in such a way as to make it impossible for him to avoid seeing it. This display caused him to be overcome by debility a second time. Upon his recovery from this attack, he was gripped by severe fever. Against the King's orders, Herr von Münchow had the window curtains lowered and sent for the doctors, who declared my brother to be very seriously ill. He refused to accept anything of all he was offered. He was beside himself and his agitation so excessive that he would have killed himself, had he been left unattended.* [22] Not until seven weeks after the execution, on December 27, 1730, was the King's minister, General Frederick William von Grumbkow, notified by fortress Küstrin: *Following three attacks, the Crown Prince's fever has subsided; however, he looks utterly wretched.* [23]

The tragic loss of his friend left a deep mark on the eighteen-year-old Crown Prince. How profoundly her brother had changed even outwardly as a result of his Küstrin experience is described by Wilhelmine in her memoirs. She herself played a decisive part in ending his imprisonment by declaring herself ready to follow her father's command and marry the Heriditary Margrave of Bayreuth, a man totally unknown to her and beneath her in rank. Frederick would regain his freedom after the fact and brother and sister finally see one another again on the occasion of her wedding festivities in November of 1731, fifteen months following her detention: *Grumbkow interrupted me in the middle of a minuet. 'But Princess,' he said, 'You seem bitten by a tarantula. Don't you see those strangers who have just arrived?' I paused, scanned the room and actually spotted a young man, completely dressed in gray, whom I did not recognize. 'Why don't you give him a hug,' he said, 'it's the Crown Prince.' My heart leapt for joy. 'Heavens!' I cried, 'my brother! But where is he? Point him out to me for God's sake!' Grumbkow led me to him. As I approached him, I recognized him but with difficulty. He had gained a good deal of weight and developed a very short neck; also his face had changed: It was no longer as handsome as it once was.* [24]

To be sure, Frederick could now move about more freely, but he had lost his sister, his closest confidante, to the Heriditary Margrave of Bayreuth. He was suitably

Wilhelmine as married Hereditary Princess of Bayreuth, painted in 1734 by Antoine Pesne. Her mother would have preferred to see her at the side of her nephew, the English Crown Prince.

subdued in his interactions with the newlyweds during the wedding festivities. Moreover, he had not yet fully regained his freedom. First there were further conditions to fulfill. Just as with his sister, his father decreed a marriage for him too: He was to marry the – in his eyes – unsympathetic Elisabeth Christine von Braunschweig-Bevern. If he wanted to be released, he had to submit. About his future wife he wrote to his sister in March of 1732, she having meanwhile moved to the court of Bayreuth: *The Princess has a very pretty face, but deep-lying eyes and an ugly mouth. She has a farmer's gait and a gaze that looks up at you … , an unpleasant laugh, a gait like a duck, bad teeth, dresses very badly, is nervous in conversation and almost always mute. Apart from that, she has a beautiful complexion, a beautiful bosom, a beautiful figure at about your height, pretty hands, blond hair, a good heart. She's not moody, but rather polite, but always too much or too little, quite modest, very poorly educated and without the slightest breeding. From this picture, dearest sister, you can tell that I don't like her at all and that I am absolutely livid over this marriage. One can see in advance that it'll be a very bad one. It often pains me, but what one cannot change, one must accept.* [25]

The wedding took place on June 12, 1733, in Salzdahlum Palace at the Braunschweig court. As early as the wedding night, the bridegroom wrote to his sister who lay ill in Berlin: *I hope to see you again soon and I can assure you that I am all yours.* [26] The Crown Prince had, of course, bowed to the inevitable, but he now avoided his wife's proximity. He was aided in this by the fact that his father, the *Soldier King*, had already appointed him colonel of an infantry regiment stationed in Nauen and Ruppin a year earlier, so that Ruppin was for the time being his rather modest residence, a place with little accommdation to offer the royal household of the Crown Princess. There he carried out his prescribed duties and drilled his regiment – when absolutely necessary. He now took joy again, as he always had, in literature and music. And so he summoned the singer and composer Carl Heinrich Graun to Ruppin in order to hone his musical and compositional skills under that man's tutelage. Music meant something more to him than to most of the higher nobility of his time, who like him sought to be esteemed as musicians and composers: It was no mere idle pastime but a means of expressing individual feeling. On March 7, 1735, he wrote to Wilhelmine:

*I take the liberty of sending you the long-promised solo. Please tell me if you like it or not. The bass is entirely by me, with not a single improvement by another's hand, for I've been studying the half notes for six weeks. With the adagio I was reminded of the long period of our separation and so was able to find the tones expressing painful lament. With the allegro the hope of our reunion quickened my spirit, and with the presto my fervid imagination transported me to Bayreuth. It was as if, all at once, I had hundreds of all manner of things to tell you, and my heart stirred up so many thoughts that each one of them, in blind rivalry, pushed forward to be the first to reach the light. As you see, dear sister, friendship in any form struggles for expression.*[27]

After the wedding, as before, Frederick was able to rouse scant affection for his consort. A next-but-one heir to the throne seemed an unlikely prospect. A few months after the wedding, following innumerable paternal exhortations (which were fruitless in the truest sense of the word), Frederick Wilhelm I presented the newlyweds with the Rheinsberg palace, which, in the opinion of the Crown Prince, needed to be expanded by Wenzeslaus von Knobelsdorff. Elisabeth Christine's dowry of 25,000 thalers was of critical assistance in the acquisition of the palace. It was there that the couple would live together and produce progeny. Since the Princess had by now learned to mingle in the social circle, living together with a court society of thirty or forty interesting personalities turned out to be unexpectedly harmonious. Yet the Rheinsberg period remained the exception; thereafter there would be no further married life between them.

The move into the palace, while still under renovation, in the summer of 1736 was for Frederick the beginning of a new intellectual and personal freedom. *Now I'm on my own country estate,* he wrote to Wilhelmine on June 7, *and take in the pleasures of country living with full drafts…. It only remains for your presence to make my happiness complete.*[28]

Animals were also part of social life at Rheinsberg, free as they were to move about unhindered in all

*Pesne summons all his art to paint a good picture of me in keeping
with your instructions. I'm constantly asking him ... to express the
feelings I cherish for you, so that they may always be present to you.*
Crown Prince Frederick to Wilhelmine, Berlin, March 10, 1736.

rooms for the pleasure of all. There was Mimi, one of the cheeky little palace monkeys, who on one occasion threw a French translation of Wolff's treatise on metaphysics into a burning fireplace, and a large poodle that a maid mistook for Herr von Bielfeld, when the latter, following a bout of excessive drinking, fell down a flight of stairs in the dark. There were other dogs too, among them a little gray-and-white-spotted Italian greyhound with clipped ears that belonged to the Crown Princess and would occasionally run away from her, as one could read about in the newspapers. Of course, at this point in time the King's attachment to the animals does not appear as yet to have been especially strong; other things were far more important to him.

Frederick turned especially to the muses and to philosophical studies. Since early youth he had been fascinated by the writings of Voltaire, and it was these to which he now devoted himself intensively in Rheinsberg. (The relationship between the French philosopher and the Prussian King, which was not always unclouded, has been treated at length in the historical literature. For Frederick, the relationship with Voltaire, as the correspondence with Wilhelmine documents, was an intellectual challenge, but not a sincere friendship. The great Enlightenment philosopher's stays in Potsdam were likely more a matter of the mutual acquisition of prestige than of interpersonal enrichment. Unlike some other personalities whose names are often associated with Frederick II, Voltaire was never an intimate of the King and for that reason plays no prominent role in the further course of this book, which seeks primarily to illuminate the King's withdrawal from people and gravitation towards his little dogs.)

The Crown Prince began a kind of general studies course, one he designed himself: *We've divided our activities into two classifications, first the utilitarian and second the agreeable. Among the utilitarian I count the study of philosophy, history and languages. The agreeable ones are music, comedies and tragedies that we put on ourselves, masquerades and mutual surprises with presents.*[29]

With great intensity he also grappled with the world-view of scholar Christian Wolff, who in the year 1723 had been removed by Frederick William I from his professorial chair under humiliating circumstances – for being *a danger to religion* – and expelled from Prussia. In Wolff's philosophy the Divine Creator is seen as the author of both good and evil. Accordingly, both are viewed as inherent in the individual soul from birth on, which is an argument against the existence of witches and devils, both of these still deeply rooted in the mindset of the eighteenth century. The course of individual moral behavior was therefore prescribed through the laws of the Creator, which were meant to keep evil under restraint and strengthen the virtues. These divine prescriptions were not only verifiable through biblical passages but could also be deduced from the perceptions of autonomous reason.

Thus Wolff's highest moral requirement could be stated as follows: *Do that which tends to perfect yourself and your condition or that of others; refrain from that which makes it less perfect.* [30] It was also this postulate to which the Crown Prince could now reconcile himself again. The Electoral Saxon envoy in Berlin, Ulrich Friedrich von Suhm, noted: *I will not further elaborate the fine qualities of this Prince. He is making a serious effort to acquire as many virtues as possible. On one occasion this prompted me to say to him that he was striving for a goal he would never reach, the goal of perfection. Whereupon he answered that the situation was much like that with the stone of wisdom: He who seeks it will be rewarded for his effort with many good things which he finds along the way.* [31]

Rheinsberg was Frederick's refuge, which, with a nod to General von Grumbkow, he was already calling *my Sanssouci.* [32] The idyll was, however, not untroubled; just as before, much had to take place in secret. Outside the palace the hated father continued to rule; even though in the meanwhile laid low with illness, he simply refused to die, as if to spite the Crown Prince's dearest wishes. In July, 1738, Frederick came into contact with people who found themselves in difficult situations similar to his own. Only clandestinely and under great threat of punishment were they able to pursue their enlightened ideals. Ethical conduct, personal development and friendship beyond all constraints of class and religion were among their essential life maxims. Following the medieval ideal of the builders united in symbolic brotherhood, they would meet in friendship lodges. The fellowship of Freemasons, originally founded in England in December of 1717, commenced activity in Germany in December, 1737, with the establishment of the first Hamburg lodge. As early as four months later, however, on April 28, 1738, membership in this union was punishable by the severest of all church penalties, that of excommunication. With his bull, *In eminenti*, Pope Clement XII forbade all *entering into the society of Freemasons, as well as propagating the society, protecting it, or receiving its members in houses or palaces.*[33] Catholic Europe in particular reacted to the despised community with dramatic persecutions, not excluding the death penalty. On July 12 it came down to the Crown Prince's first personal encounter with a Freemason, and that in his father's presence. At a banquet following a review of the troops in Minden, the King spoke out against the brotherhood with great vehemence. It came then as a complete surprise when he was resolutely contradicted by the reigning Count Albrecht Wolfgang zu Schaumburg-Lippe, who finally summoned the courage to declare before Frederick Wilhelm I that he himself was a Freemason. This courageous confession must have deeply impressed the Crown Prince, who had so often been forced to deny his own interests before the King. Ignoring all personal risk, he made the decision to join this alliance that shared his enlightened ideals as quickly as possible as a private citizen.

As early as the night from August 14 to 15, Frederick, in a deviation from the usual order of rank, was directly appointed, neither an apprentice nor a journeyman, but a *Worshipful Master,* enabling him to preside over his own lodge. That lodge's founding followed in the Fall of 1739 in Rheinsberg, where he himself accepted lodge brothers. Among these were numbered Baron von Keyserlingk, Wenzeslaus von Knobelsdorff, Charles Etienne Jordan and Michael Gabriel Fredersdorf.

These experiences of the Crown Prince now found expression even in the artistic refurbishing of the Rheinsberg estate. In similar fashion, in 1739 he had the largest hall of the palace decorated with paintings depicting hopeful motifs. As lodge brother Baron Jacob Frederick von Bielfeld, a visitor at Rheinsberg, noted: *The renowned Pesne is right now painting the ceiling fresco. It depicts sunrise. On one side night is fleeing, shrouded in her veil, surrounded by those eerie birds of hers and followed by her Horae, in order to make room for the dawn, which occupies the middle of the ceiling and is accompanied by the morning star in the figure of Venus.*[34]

A few months later, on May 31, 1740, Frederick William I died. The Crown Prince, as Frederick II, now became King in Prussia.

# IV
*Conquering Anxiety and Enduring Illness*
The Period of the Silesian Wars
(1740-1745)

*My youth was a school of suffering.* Thus Frederick's summary as monarch. *Unhappiness has always pursued me. Only in Rheinsberg have I been happy.* [35] After his dramatic experiences he had found a true confidant in the extremely unconventional Baron von Keyserlingk. *He declared openly,* said the Saxon privy councilor Johann Ulrich of the Prussian heir apparent, *that it was thanks solely and exclusively to the Cavalry Captain von Keyserlingk that, as Crown Prince, he did not fall prey to complete despair in his persecution during that period. Keyserlingk was the one who, through his cheerful disposition and his lofty sentiments, encouraged him to practice equanimity in his suffering and the magnanimous overcoming of his evil star.* [36] Since Rheinsberg, the cavalry captain also looked after the Italian greyhounds living at court. Six weeks after Frederick's accession to the throne, the newsletter for 11 July 1740 reported: *Lost: one English little greyhound, brown and white, female. Whoever delivers same to the Adjutant General or to Colonel Baron von Keyserling [sic] can expect generous compensation for himself from His Majesty's suite.* [37]

Next to Baron von Keyserlingk, Michael Gabriel Fredersdorf, who had already been first valet to the Crown Prince in Rheinsberg, and Count von Rothenburg

Dietrich Baron von Keyserlingk, here in a painting by Antoine Pesne from the year 1738, would go on hunts in his dressing gown with his musket and would abruptly perform dance movements before speaking on politics, painting, philosophy or even warfare – at least in the summer of 1739 upon meeting with Herr von Bielfeld in Rheinsberg.

became increasingly more important. They also played a special role in connection with the King's love of Italian greyhounds. It was Count Rothenburg who gave him his first pet dog, *Biche*. Frederick had known the Count, only a year and a half older than himself, since his crown-prince period and called him to Berlin after becoming king on June 1, 1740. Frederick Rudolf Count von Rothenburg was an extraordinary personality who also made an attractive appearance. Already at fourteen he had commenced a program of study at the University of Frankfurt (Oder), transferring, however, as a devotee of French culture, to Lunéville a year later. In 1727 he entered French military service as Captain of the Rosen Infantry Regiment, fighting in North Africa, and was in Spain on a diplomatic mission. In 1733 this count, descended from an age-old Silesian noble family, converted to Catholicism. He was one of those natures Frederick liked having in his personal entourage on account of their self-reliance. For his own part, Count Rothenburg admired Frederick II as an enlightened monarch, who, even in the first month of his accession to the throne, undertook immense changes throughout the land. Within the first few days numerous cabinet orders were decreed. First, the King had grain released from state storehouses at minimal prices to a populace that was starving for it following a failed harvest. One day later, on June 3, the rack was abolished in Prussia. On June 6 the King called the philosopher Christian Wolff back to Prussian service. Forcible recruitment was forbidden. Prussian soldiers would receive better treatment from then on. Compulsory building was repealed. The Academy of Sciences was revived. An opera company in Italy and a theater troupe in Paris were hired. Finally, on June 22 Frederick proclaimed his principles of religious freedom: *All religions must*

*be tolerated and the Crown must keep a sharp eye out*
*that one religion does not harm another, for here each*
*person must attain salvation by his own lights.*[38]

Enlightened Europe, to which Rothenburg too belonged, was inspired by these developments in Prussia. The Count entered the Prussian army as a Colonel and immediately proved to be of great assistance in the First Silesian War, which the King waged against the new Empress on the Habsburg throne. The coming to power of the Archduchess Maria Theresa of Austria, Queen of both Bohemia and Hungary, on October 20, 1740, was a welcome occasion for the Prussian ruler to make demands on rich and heavily populated Silesia, demands he had already established as Crown Prince with a position paper of the Great Elector. The conquest of Silesia also appealed to the Great Elector in his role as defender of religious freedom as a way of supporting its Protestant residents, who he believed to be oppressed by their lack of territorial sovereignty. Furthermore, the King saw himself as quite in accord with the will of his deceased father. Frederick William I had suffered in many ways from the disdain of the House of Habsburg, but did not see himself as being in a position to respond adequately to the injustice perpetrated against him. Now his son set about settling old accounts. In doing so he also succeeded in elevating himself above his father as a politician and, above all, as a field commander.[39] All conditions for an attack seemed favorable to Frederick. He had taken over from his father a militarily strong state, whereas Austria had been weakened, having in 1739 lost Serbia and Wallachia in a war against the Turks. In addition, Carl Albrecht of Bavaria, Philip V of Spain and Frederick August of Saxony staked claims to the thrones of the Austrian heredity lands, since they did not recognize the Pragmatic Sanction by which Maria Theresa's father, Emperor Charles VI, had established accession to the throne even in the female lineage. On December 13, 1740, the King left Berlin. On the 16th he marched with his troops into Silesia. The First Silesian War had begun.

At first, the advance of Prussian troops met with little resistance, since those under attack were unprepared. However, two months later, in February of 1741, the King fell into mortal danger near Liegnitz with the revelation of enemy positions through reconnaissance. Finally, at the beginning of April, the Austrian army reached Silesia under the supreme command of Count William Reinhard von Neipperg. Just before the Battle of Mollwitz, the first serious confrontation with the Austrians, Frederick declared his last will and testament. In this disposition, which, in view of his own childlessness, he conveyed to the brother nearest him in age as heir apparent, the King remembered the individuals who made up his inner circle. On April 8, 1741, he wrote to Prince August William:

*Dearest brother. The enemy has just moved into Silesia. We stand opposite him a quarter mile away. Tomorrow will decide our fate. If I should fall, do not forget a brother who has always loved you tenderly. With my dying breath I commend to you my beloved mother, my servants and my first Battalion Guard. ... Remember me always, but console yourself over my sacrifice. The splendor of Prussian weapons and the honor of our house determine my conduct and will guide me even unto death. You are my only heir. If I die, I commend to you those whom I have loved most in life: Keyserlingk, Jordan, Wartensleben, Hacke, who is a man of honor, Fredersdorf and Eichel, whom you can fully trust. Eight thousand thalers, which I have on my person, I bequeath to my servants; however, everything else that I possess depends on you. Make a gift to all my brothers and sisters in my name; extend to my sister in Bayreuth a thousand heartfelt* greetings. *You know what I think of her, and, better than I am able to say it, you know the love and all the feelings of the most steadfast friendship with which I forever remain.*

*Your loyal brother and servant unto death, Frederick.*[40]

Count Rothenburg went unmentioned in this testament. His importance to the young King would first become apparent in the battle that was imminent, in which he would remain close by his side. The horror of war taught Frederick that it was not words but deeds that distinguished the true friend. In the same vein, in 1741 he had summoned a small group of the Rheinsberg court society to his encampment at Breslau. As enemy troops moved closer, these theoretical apologists for a stoic composure were overcome by the sheer fear of death. The King took this sobering experience as

Count Rothenburg shared the King's interest in the revolutionary game of chess, in which the pawns, and not the upper classes, were at the center of warfare. (Oil painting by Antoine Pesne)

evidence for the argument that titans of the scholarly study prove in the end to be no more than frightened little frauds. Nevertheless, he remained favorably disposed towards them; his fearful companions of youth, Baron von Keyserlingk and Charles Etienne Jordan, would continue to count among his most intimate circle. Despite their human weaknesses, they were irreplaceable to him. He owed them a great deal and required, especially in hard times, their intellectual stimulation, their esprit and their friendly affection. But he no longer took them seriously as political advisors. He reserved his deepest respect for those who could stand by his side in more than trivial situations; among these Count Rothenburg certainly belonged. In the Battle of Chotusitz in May, 1742, against Prince Carl von Lothringen, Maria Theresa's brother-in-law, he fought at the head of the troops of Prince August William. By virtually destroying the Austrians' Schönberg regiment, he ushered in Frederick's victory. This led to the Preliminary Peace of Breslau and finally to the Peace of Berlin, which forced Maria Theresa to cede Upper and Lower Silesia as well as the county of Glatz. The weak wartime conduct and poor cooperation of his alliance partners France, Saxony and Bavaria had primed Frederick's readiness to enter into negotiations with Austria – in part, behind the backs of his allies. On July 2, 1742, he wrote to his sister Wilhelmine from Brieg, *It is gratifying to be able to tell you that I have concluded a peace with the Queen of Hungary. The lack of good will from the French, the disloyalty of the Saxons and a plethora of similar reasons have forced me to do it.*[41]

The Treaty of Berlin represented a blatant breach of trust towards France, which continued the War of Succession against Austria, a war Holland and England also entered in 1743 on the side of Maria Theresa. Based on the balance of power in Europe that was shifting against his interests, it became essential for the King to renew his alliance with the French, whom he had snubbed. For this task too Count Rothenburg, who had once served in the French army, seemed to him the most suitable negotiator. In February, 1774, Rothenburg went to Paris on a diplomatic mission, where, moreover, his wife was living, she being the daughter of French Lieutenant-General Marquis de Parabère. As son-in-law of the Marquise Marie-Madeleine de Parabère, he possessed valuable contacts in court society. The Marquise had in younger years been the mistress of Philipp of Orleans (d. 1723), who upon the death of Louis XIV in September of 1715 had been appointed by parliament as regent. These family connections proved to be extremely helpful. The alliance between France and Brandenburg-Prussia was accomplished on June 5, 1744.

The Count also used his sojourn in Paris to acquire French art for the King. On March 30, 1744, he bought two pictures by the painter Lancret and shortly thereafter two smaller and – after a long search – a further large painting by Antoine Watteau, since the King wanted three large pictures by the prematurely deceased (d. 1721) painter for his newly emerging residence, Sanssouci. The paintings in question were *The Love Lesson*, *French Comedians* and *The Shop Sign of the Art Dealer Gersaint*. Interestingly, dogs frequently play a not insignificant commenting role in the depictions of this artist who was already highly esteemed in the 18th century. In Gersaint's art gallery a dog delouses

Dogs in their guilelessness became in some Watteauian paintings commentators on the Rococo scenarios, such as here in *The Shepherds* (ca. 1717)

itself in front of an idle company. In the painting *The Shepherds*, already three years in the King's possession, a small animal occupies itself unashamedly with its better half, while the couples shown are still in the flirtation stage. In *The Love Lesson*, an elegantly poetic painting, sitting at the feet of a young lady as she views some music sheets is a dwarf spaniel resembling Wilhelmine's Folichon that is the only one gazing in the viewer's direction. Certainly these striking details did not escape the attention of the King and his envoy in Paris, for both had by this time already developed a strong affinity for dogs. Count Rothenburg had meanwhile presented Frederick with the Italian she-greyhound *Biche*, who was also to be portrayed as part of a mythological painting for the music room in Sanssouci palace – though not as a marginal figure like the dogs in Watteau's pictures, but together with Diana, goddess of the hunt, in the center of the painting. By now this dog occupied such a place in the King's life. She was allowed to accompany him to the cure at Bad Pyrmont, where Frederick intended to prepare himself for the next armed engagement. This last seemed to him unavoidable after learning that England, in a secret pact, had recognized Austria's boundaries as they were before the First Silesian War. Since Maria Theresa's cession of Silesia to Prussia was thereby invalidated, the King had decided to reenter the War of Austrian Succession, which had continued without interruption since 1742.

In the spring of 1744, not only were political tensions in Europe escalating, but conflicts in the King's family were building as well. For the first time he had a falling-out with his sister Wilhelmine, to whom he imputed sympathies for Austria because of her friendly disposition towards Maria Theresa. The customary intimate communication between them now belonged to the past.

On April 29 Wilhelmine wrote to Frederick: *The letter written to me by my brother William* (August William), *at your behest, affected me painfully. I would never have thought it possible that you could treat so harshly a sister who has loved you as I have and who* has never once missed an opportunity to prove it to you. If you take even the slightest joy in being loved by me, then you must behave differently towards me, for I have done nothing to you for which to reproach myself; I am ever prepared, and will always remain so, to shed my blood for you.[42]

The King replied:
*Dear sister! An old saw says one should judge people by their deeds, not by their words. If this is true, then you can easily imagine what I must think of your deed. I will not go into details and can tell you no more than that I remain, etc. … I'm going to the baths; it is forbidden for me to write from there.*[43]

Undeterred, Wilhelmine turned to him again:
*Hermitage, May 22, 1744*
*It was with endless joy that I received your last letter. Despite its coldness it pacified my heart again, which was inconsolable over the loss of your friendship. You say, dearest brother, one should show one's disposition through deeds. My God, have I not then given you sufficient proof of my love? And can this recently occurring history by itself cause you to forget all else? … I pray to heaven that the bathwaters in Pyrmont are as agreeable to you as possible. I'm well aware that one is not permitted to write during the cure, but one may read, and so I will permit myself to write to you as often as possible.*[44]

The King used the journey to Pyrmont as a preparation for war. Consequently, the stay there was marked by great unrest. On May 25 the last ruler of the principality of East Frisia died. Through quick occupation of the region, the King established Prussian hereditary title, avoiding all disputes with Hanover in doing so. In the further course of his stay at the health spa and most importantly, Frederick ratified a treaty of alliance with Bavaria, the Palatinate and Hesse-Kassel, and on June 5, as previously mentioned, his alliance with France was again reinforced by Count Rothenburg. On the diplomatic level, the cure was for Frederick a great success – but his health as well seemed to have profited from the sojourn. Attesting to this is a report of June 5 form the cure physician Dr. Seip to his superior authority: *His Royal Majesty the King of Prussia has as of today drunk [the waters] for 14 days and bathed in them 6 times, finds himself well, thank God, and quite cheerful, staying on here till the afternoon of June 9, when He will leave straightaway for Potsdam.*[45]

Three weeks later, on June 30, 1744, the events for which Frederick had prepared himself during his stay at the spa occurred. Maria Theresa's forces crossed the Rhine with 70,000 men, intending to invade Alsace. Now the King acted, as he himself expressed it, for the protection of German freedoms and for the protection of Silesia. The Second Silesian War had begun.

In mid-August, 1744, the Prussian army began to move, via Dresden, towards Prague, its destination. Among those most closely accompanying the King was the little she-dog *Biche*. The fortress of Prague, defended by a mere 14,000 men, surrendered following a short siege. Alas, his military position changed significantly as the King advanced along the Danube towards Vienna. Maria Theresa now successfully turned all available forces against him. Decimated in numbers by a quarter, plagued by dysentery, typhus and desertion, Prussian troops were finally even forced to give up Prague. Frederick, standing on an existential precipice, decided against his advisers, all of whom were pressing for rapprochement, in favor of another battle, seemingly with little prospect for success. Appealing tirelessly to the fighting spirit of his demoralized troops, he drew up a cunning battle plan on his own. The unimaginable happened: the Prussians prevailed at Hohenfriedberg, on June 4, 1745. Shortly thereafter, on June 10, the King wrote to his maternal friend, Countess Camas, his senior by twenty-six years: *We had more luck than brains. The loving God clearly took us to his bosom, and it is to the multitude of good and brave officers that I owe all my good fortune.* [46]

One month later he learned of the death of his dear friend Keyserlingk. Just before that, in May, Charles Etienne Jordan, his literary and philosophical mentor, had passed away. On August 30, from the encampment near Semonitz, he turned once again to Countess Camas:

*The last time I wrote you, I was in a quite tranquil mood and did not foresee the adversity that was to strike me. In less than three months I have lost my best, most loyal friends, people with whom I have always lived and who, through my comforting association with them, their character as honorable men and the genuine friendship I had with them, often helped me to conquer anxiety and endure illness. You can judge for yourself: For a heart that is made so soft as mine, it is hard to stifle the deep pain this loss causes me. On my return to Berlin, I will feel virtually foreign in my own native city and lonely among my own Penates, so to speak. I speak here to a person who gave proof of her steadfastness when she lost, also practically with one blow, so many people who were dear to her, but I confess to you I admire your courage without being able to emulate it. I place my only hope in a time that will make an end of all that exists in nature and that will therewith begin to weaken our mental life, in order then to destroy us utterly.* [47]

Frederick could in fact only count on the healing of his wounds over time. He was the King and it was wartime. There was scarcely room for him to indulge his grief; he had to be a paragon for his officers and the challenges only increased. Perhaps it was *Biche*, whoprobably trembling herself from fear in the encampment – offered him consolation in her own way. At the very least, he had never before given an animal such loving attention. She was permitted to accompany him everywhere, even into battle. Despite

*Biche, however, as though sensing her master's plight, pressed herself tightly against him and made not a sound.* Woodcut by A. W. Wachsmann, *Friedrich II. mit seinem Lieblingshund Biche.*

her gentleness, she would be the one to prove herself one of those companions he could trust even in danger. This became apparent no more than a month later when master and dog fell into a precarious situation together. The unexpected appearance of enemy troops almost became a trap for both of them. Frederick had assessed the situation incorrectly in expecting the end of positional warfare, including the withdrawal of both armies to their respective winter quarters, too soon. He was therefore unprepared for the immediately impending Battle of Soor on September 30, 1745. He had already substantially weakened his army in favor of the troops under Prince Leopold von Anhalt-Dessau that were standing ready near Halle to fight Saxony, since he was hoping for imminent peace negotiations led by England. Maria Theresa, however, was not willing to accept peace without the return of Silesia. The war continued. Shortly after the King occupied his headquarters in Rohnstock, the Austrian army approached the Prussian encampment. This event is reported by the biographer Franz Kugler: *On one occasion Frederick risked advancing too far on a reconnaissance mission; suddenly he spotted a contingent of Pandurs riding towards him on the road; he had no choice but to jump down into a trench and hide under a bridge. But now he was afraid that Biche, who was with him, might start barking at the noise of the horses' hooves, thereby giving him away; the animal, however, as though sensing the danger to his master, snuggled up to him closely and didn't make a sound.*[48]

Once the King realized the danger presented by the amassing enemy troops, he decided on a surprise attack, and triumphed. However, the losses were immense; even his own headquarters were raided and plundered by the Hungarian General Radasdy. Once again the little dog was involved in the events. Frederick wrote to his brother, August William: *On September 30, 1745, Radasdy robbed me of my English little greyhound, called Biche, who was being kept by my servant Klaus.*[49] He described the entire disaster to his close friend Fredersdorf in greater detail. The letter, composed in an awkward German for his *factotum* who spoke no French, is among the rare correspondence of the King in German. He wrote all other letters exclusively in a refined French, owing to his deficient mastery of the German language. First of all, in his letter to Fredersdorf, he bemoaned the presumed death of the horses *Annemarie* and *Champion* as well as his dog *Biche*. After that he reported on officers missing in action, the serious injuries to Count Rothenburg and the death of Prince Albert, the brother of his wife, Queen Elisabeth Christine, whom he apparently did not particularly esteem: *Just imagine the fight: eighteen against fifty! All my equipment shot to hell, Annemarie hacked to death, Champion and Biche*[50] *probably also dead; Eichel, Müller, the cipher clerk and Lesser have not been found yet. Once misfortune sets its sights, it'll ride your back every time. ... The campaign is now surely over and I'll be able to end it whenever I please. Just stay calm! Rothenburg could easily have died; Knobelsdorff came back 1st. Brave, good Wedell is dead; Albert too, though that's no great loss. ... Heaven help us. Never in all my days have I been in such great danger and distress than on the 30th, and yet I came through it!*[51]

Fortunately, *Biche* was not dead; she would be at Frederick's side again in just a few days. There are at least two versions of the order of events in this reunion. As Johannes Richter, editor of the King's correspondence with Fredersdorf, tells it: *But upon repeated requests the animal was given back. It is said that they quietly let Biche into the room where the King was writing letters. The dog jumped up onto the table and placed its paws around its master's neck; the King was so happy*

*that tears came to his eyes.*[52] The biographer Friedrich
Rudolf Paulig writes: *A few days after the battle he*
*was sitting at his desk. Biche had kept searching over*
*a distance of many miles until she found the King's*
*headquarters. She jumped unnoticed onto the King's*
*chair and expressed her joy. Frederick was so happily*
*surprised by the unexpected reunion that tears came*
*to his eyes.*[53]

Normally Frederick would have confided his personal experiences to Wilhelmine, but in view of their
strained relationship he preferred for the time being
other intimates, such as Fredersdorf, who had long ac-
quitted himself well at court but also, and especially,
as a friend. During his imprisonment in Küstrin, Frederick had made the acquaintance of this son of a poor
town musician. Due to his considerable size, the four-
year-older Michael Gabriel Fredersdorf had originally
been recruited by agents of the *Soldier King*. Even in
the fortress he had been a great help to the detainee:
Risking mortal danger he had carried the latter's secret
letters to Wilhelmine and to Queen Sophie Dorothea.
Also, he loved music and played the flute, as did the
Crown Prince. When Frederick was released from the
fortress prison, his first order of business was to make
Fredersdorf his valet. Upon his accession to the throne
in 1740, he rose to the rank of Privy Chamberlain, or
keeper of the royal coffers. It was with this intimate
of many years that Frederick, about one month after
the Battle of Soor, shared the most private thoughts

and feelings he had had during the war: *I'm very concerned about my health; I can't sleep at night because of heart palpitations and cramping colitis and can only eat very little. Now, with everything calm and quiet, I know I need something, but I'm worried that I'll be spending the winter with many incommodities; all the colds, worries and sorrows are completely ruining me.*[54]

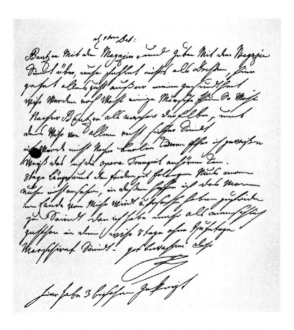

*... have gotten 3 pups here.* Facsimile of Frederick II's letter of December 1, 1745, to his dear friend Fredersdorf.

In a letter written two days later, he reports to him about all his struggles during the war and about the threefold litter of his she-dog *Biche*, who, happily, had made it back to camp.

*(Görlitz) Dec. 1 (1745)*
*… Everything is going well here, except for my health. We'll probably do a few more marches, first to Bautzen and then to the Elbe, in order to be sure of everything. I will not be able to return to Berlin unless I know for sure that I can hear the opera Tranquil. … Meanwhile, I hope that people around the country will have good reason to be satisfied with me, as I've done all that is humanly possible, having marched 8 days without a day of rest. God bless you!*
*Have gotten 3 pups here.*[55]

Three difficult weeks were yet to pass before the hoped-for rest. Following the Victory at Kesseldorf, the peace treaty with Austria and Saxony was signed on Christmas Day. In it the Habsburgs reaffirmed Prussia's Silesian holdings, already acknowledged in 1742 in the Peace of Breslau, and, as a quid pro quo, the Prussian King relinquished his territorial gains in Bohemia and Silesia. In addition, Frederick was prepared to accept Maria Theresa's husband, Franz I, as Holy Roman Emperor. When the King returned to Berlin on December 28, 1745, he was given a spirited welcome by the populace and celebrated as victor in the Second Silesian War – and, for the first time, honored with the epithet *the Great*.

# V

*Happy He Who Comes to Peace through Wisdom*
Years of Peace in Sanssouci
(1746-1751)

Over the years, Frederick developed a quite stinging, but also humorous way of dealing with his circle of friends and associates. During a second stay at the health spa in Bad Pyrmont, six months after the end of the war, he expressed the wish for his chamberlain, Karl Ludwig von Pöllnitz, and his twenty-year-old brother Heinrich, who felt drawn rather to the young men than the ladies, to drink the healing Pyrmont waters. His pronouncement on the subject was, however, not especially discreet. Upon observing the King, the son-in-law of the treating spa doctor noted the following with astonishment on June 8, 1746:

*The King likes to joke with people. Once in the garden he said to both physicians that Prince Heinrich, who was present, should drink the well water so that he can marry, and Pöllnitz so that he'll learn to pay his debts. He said he had observed this sort of banter on other occasions and wondered whether it was usual for the King to relate to his people that way. Among other things, when his dog had a litter three days before his departure, he gave the order to notify his Privy Chamberlain Fredersdorf, just now taking the cure at Aachen, of the fact and send him a letter from the godfather, appending the remark that he should visit the puerpera with her young.*[56]

Frederick used words to create distance; he had long been feared as a cynic. But then, was the source of this cynicism not perhaps a frustrated desire for deeper friendship? Psychoanalytic theory at least suggests such an interpretative approach. A letter written by Frederick on August 30, 1746, shortly after his stay in Pyrmont, to the heir apparent, August William, ten years his junior, seems to support this thesis: *Dear brother! … The main thing in life is to be self-sufficient, for one can only rely on oneself. Our friends die before us or are far away, or one does not wish to become a burden to them. So one is thrown back on one's own resources. To find support and consolation, one must occasionally, by careful selection, sort out the best from our old and new authors.*

*… Biche's pups are doing very well.*[57]

This is not to say, however, that there were only negative interpersonal outcomes in the King's life. By virtue of the peace agreement implemented on the European political stage, it now became easier for Frederick in the private sphere as well to improve his relationship with his sister Wilhelmine. After the end of the Second Silesian War, brother and sister drew closer together following a frank discussion by letter. Both were extremely happy over the reconciliation – just how happy may be seen in an affectionate letter from the now thirty-eight-year-old Wilhelmine to her brother. For its form she chose a fictive missive written by her dwarf spaniel *Folichon* to Frederick's dog *Biche*.

*Bayreuth, May 1748*
*Folichon to Biche*

*Admit, dear Biche, that humans are very foolish, and very little conscious of being so. … Aren't you as amazed as I am by the plethora of philosophers who have undertaken to fathom our nature while having not the slightest idea what they themselves are. … Except for our shape, are we then not exactly like humans? Are not our passions the same? Love, jealousy, anger and gluttonousness are as much our tyrants as theirs. The only difference is this: We possess fewer vices and more virtues. Humans are thoughtless, fickle, selfish and overambitious; these defects are unknown to us. Rather we possess loyalty, constancy, devotion and gratitude, qualities that are almost banned from society. Can one find truer friends than us? Our friendship for our masters is unalterable and abiding, in their greatness as in their baseness. Consequently, humans should take us as a model, instead of despising us. Forgive this long discourse; it is only the introduction to a more compelling subject. You, revered Biche, have brought up all these thoughts in me; their basis is my love for you. Yes, dearest dog, I love and revere you. Your spirit, your grace, a thousand qualities that shine in you, have conquered me. Ah, I burst into tears when I think of the sweet little way you stroked me with your paw when I took that ill-fated leave of you. How much more sincere than the so-called rational species, you showed me your true feelings and said to me, "I love you, dear Folichon." And so, since our separation I have longed only for you. Gaunt and drooping, I spend my time dejected at my mistress's feet. I've been listening to her complain of her terrible separation from a beloved brother and talk endlessly about the happy time she spent with him in Berlin, without being able to take part in her conversations. Concerned about my distress and in order to restore my good humor, she has given me a harem of the most beautiful she-dogs in the land. Yet in vain! I scorned them all. Finally she hoped to banish my sadness with the charms of wealth. Would you believe, adored one, that that very self-interest to which we are so little subject brought about in me what the most alluring caresses and friends were not able to? Surveying my mistress's rich bounty, I immediately decided to offer it to you. At least, so I told myself, my beautiful Biche will think of me whenever she rests on these pillows. She will drink to my health from this bowl and perhaps shed a few tears over my absence.*

*Jumping and hopping around, I immediately asked my good mistress, who understands my language perfectly, to fulfill my wishes. I dictated this letter to her. Out of friendship for me she has taken great pains.*

*Receive then, beloved Biche, this small gift, which gladdens me only because it is meant for you. As you rest on this pillow, think now and then of your loyal Folichon, who will always love and treasure you and wag his tail a hundred times a day – in your honor and praise.*

*Folichon*[58]

Wilhelmine's pooch Folichon was immortalized by Wilhelm Ernst Wunder in a ceiling fresco in the Old Music Room of the Bayreuth palace.

Frederick answered in his dog's name:
*Biche to Folichon*
*I am not accustomed to receiving such gallantry. I have always adhered to the strict chastity of the ladies of my country and to romantic nobility, with the exception of a modest adventure that was ruined by my bodice; but I forgive Folichon what I would not forgive a bourgeois dog. The great love of my master for your mistress impels me to take one and only one dog as a lover. Yes, Folichon, I accept not only your gifts but your charming paw as well, and it is all the more willingly that I give you my heart, as I have long been of the opinion that a philosophical pooch suits me best. To my great astonishment I saw that my master, who read your letter to me, is totally of your opinion. He is almost as rational as we are, with a sensible head on his shoulders. But I must take*

Based on the silver letters on its collar, this Italian greyhound could be one of Frederick the Great's dogs, perhaps Thisbe or Biche. At least, the painting was thus listed in Antoine Pesne's catalogue of works in 1958 and remained so until most recently. It seems, however, to have been a much earlier work by I. C. Merck, painted by him on commission from King Frederick I, who had died in 1713.

*issue with one thing in your letter: To be sure, you have humiliated the narcissism of humans, who are so full of arrogance and vanity, but you failed to except your mistress. Yes, Folichon, say what you will, I have seen this admirable mistress, and you will never convince me that she is not of a far higher species than we. She possesses divine virtues, so much kindness, constancy, humanity and altruism that I must confess it exceeds my understanding. As you know, we can link only very few thoughts together. You, my master and I – we are cut from the same cloth; it is only out of indolence and because he does not wish to walk on all fours that my master does not call himself a dog. His nastiness classifies him as an Epicurean; an Epicurean is not far removed from a Cynic, and "kuon" in Greek means "dog." How different your mistress is! How kind she was to my master and me! How brilliant her conversation was! And her indefinable grace, her dignity, mellowed by affability, causes me to regard her as entirely admirable. Please, lay me down at her feet, and my master before me. He speaks to me only about her; it is getting hard enough for me to comfort him this winter. … God, what would become of us without ardor! Our life would be but a lingering dying; in this world we would merely be semi-conscious like the plants that live joylessly and die painlessly. Now that I love, I perceive a new world; the air I breathe is gentler, the sun shines more brilliantly, and all of nature is more alive. But, charming Folichon, are we to find our joy only in hoping? Should we not transfer to reality that which shapes the wish of our heart and the goal of our wishes? Must we be as foolish as these humans? They nourish themselves with wishes and live on fantasies, and while they waste their time on vain schemes, death seizes them from behind and sweeps them away with all their schemes. Let us be wiser than that; let us not chase after the shadow but rather seize the thing itself. I give you this trinket in pledge of my word and as a sign that I will always remain*

*Your faithful*
*Biche.*[59]
*7 June, 1748*

*Dearest brother! The gracious Biche has written to Fo-*
*lichon. What did I not feel while reading that letter! As*
*that dear animal assures me, you think of me often, my*
*absence causes you pain, and you continue to cherish*
*that precious friendship for me that has always formed*
*my happiness. She accompanies all of this with the fin-*
*est gallantry expressed through mementos, which she*
*sends to her dear Folichon. Truly, dear brother, I pre-*
*fer Biche's letters to all the epistles of Cicero, to all our*
*own jewels of eloquence, and relish them more than*
*all our old and new writers. The reason is simple: They*
*speak to me of you and your feelings for me; they cause*
*a lovely contentment to stream into my heart, which*
*alone can make us happy. For happiness, as I see it,*
*consists in the exchange of sentiments with people we*
*love. The smallest response from you suffices me. Please*
*preserve your precious kindness towards me.*[60]

*Sanssouci, 15 June 1748*
*Dearest sister! I am glad that Folichon was not offended*
*by Biche's impetuousness and that he is magnanimous*
*enough to look amiably upon her letter and her gift. Ani-*
*mals are often of use to us in that they express our sen-*
*timents more naturally and openly. La Fontaine, who*
*wrote such lovely animal fables, knew this well, and so*
*the animals to whom he gave his eloquence have taught*
*us humans a moral that few of us, alas, put into practice.*
*Biche has a healthy mind and grasp of things; every day*
*I see people who behave less consequently than she does.*
*If this dog has divined the feelings of my heart, she has*

*at least reproduced them not at all badly, and it would mean even more to me if you believed in that.*[61]

For years dogs had been constant companions of brother and sister, and so it is not surprising that Frederick and Wilhelmine should have had their pets immortalized in paintings, just as they had witnessed in youth with the Queen Mother. *Biche, Thisbe* and *Folichon* were painted by the court painter Antoine Pesne, who had been in the employ of the royal family for two generations. In 1750 he painted the by-now forty-one-year-old Wilhelmine in pilgrim's garb with Folichon in her arm. Her right hand, which thirty-five years earlier had enclosed the hand of her little brother in the siblings' double portrait, now holds a book on friendship, one that had helped to stamp the sentimentalist cult of friendship in the eighteenth century, the *Traité de l'Amitié* by Louis de Sacy. The work, published in 1703, was actually in the Margravine's extensive library. She too considered friendship to be the highest good. In the painting she sits in a kind of grotto surrounded by music sheets, a painter's palette and books, gazing seriously and pensively in the direction of the viewer. In contrast to the pleasure-oriented courtly society of her time, to which Wilhelmine in time also consigned her husband, who had for years compromised her with his mistress, Wilhelmine von der Marwitz, she devoted herself with deep seriousness to self-improvement as composer, painter and philosopher. Inspired by the intellectual exchange with her brother, she established

In the picture's year of origin, the margravial couple visited the King in Berlin and Potsdam, where Voltaire was also staying. Wilhelmine used the visit to adapt his tragedy *Semiramis* to an opera. Antoine Pesne painted Margravine Wilhelmine in pilgrim's garb in 1750.

a kind of Court of the Muses in Bayreuth. Even the costume in which Pesne painted her with its pilgrim's scallops was an expression of her interior attitude. The pilgrim's scallop served as a badge of recognition of those returning from the grave of St. James in Santiago de Compostela. Indeed, Wilhelmine saw herself as a pilgrim on the path towards enlightened ideals and virtues. In consequence, at the beginning of the 1740's, she, along with her husband, turned to the Freemasons, this at the urging of her brother. From the moment on July 9, 1740, when the King publicly proclaimed himself a Freemason in the *Journal de Berlin*, and at the same time identified by name all other members of the Rheinsberg court lodge, Masonic lodges in Prussia were no longer secret associations. Also, in October, 1740, Frederick accepted his brother-in-law into the Society, along with other family members, the former, for his part, becoming in turn co-initiator for the Bayreuth, or South German, Freemasonry contingent. Since Freemasonry was initially a strictly male domain, it was not until 1742 that it became possible for Wilhelmine to join a lodge of her own, this with the founding of the *Mopsorden* (Order of the Pug), which, as a friendship lodge, stood open to men and women of all ranks. The growing popularity of the little pug dog in the latter half of the eighteenth century, loved for its loyalty and courageousness, was directly connected with the naming of the order and also paralleled Wilhelmine's own affection for dogs. That same year the Margravine founded a lodge of the order in Bayreuth, which she also presided over as Grand Master. Wilhelmine's costume in the painting could thus be a reference to her activity on behalf of the order.[62] With this picture Pesne had once again created a portrait that went far beyond a purely decorative style of painting, succeeding as it did in expressing something fundamental. The King himself was moved by this image of his sister and selected it nineteen years later as a model for a marble statue to stand in the center of the Temple of Friendship, which he had erected in her honor in Sanssouci Park.

Meanwhile, Antoine Pesne had become a painter in demand beyond the precincts of the court. As Friedrich Rudolf Paulig says, at that time in Berlin it was *fashionable to have oneself painted by Pesne. Ladies of the genteel world gave the artist all the business he could handle. According to his address book of 1744, he lived in the house at Oberwallstraße 3. He drew a yearly salary of eleven hundred thalers. Pesne painted the entire court, and whoever sat for him was always represented in the same manner. Thus his portraits also have great value for the historian. His masterful creations hang in the galleries of Berlin, Dresden, Potsdam, Sanssouci, Salzdahlum … to the end of his life his forte was and remained the portrait.*[63]

But his murals were also of high quality, as demonstrated in his first works in Rheinsberg. These led to Pesne's being commissioned to design the wall and ceiling panels for the Sanssouci summer residence. Prince August William, who was also a great admirer of the painter, wrote to his brother on November 20, 1746: *I've seen the plans for the pictures Pesne is painting for your vineyard house. They seem to me to be in extremely good taste.*[64] The design of the concert hall was also especially noteworthy because it was precisely here that the King's love for his dogs found artistic expression. Music too had great emotional significance in Frederick's life. The time before dinner was given to concerts in which he himself played the flute. He preferred his own compositions – for his transverse flutes he wrote 121 sonatas and 4 concertos – or the works of the composer Johann Joachim Quantz, whom he had called to the Prussian court in 1741 as teacher, chamber musician and court composer.

In the concert hall of the palace, Pesne executed an ensemble of five mural paintings with mythological figures, these according to the King's guidelines. Frederick was a great connoisseur and admirer of antiquity. Not myths per se, but particular protagonists were depicted in the paintings in a new and different atmosphere. In 1747, for his magnum opus, Pesne created *Diana's Bath* on the rear wall of the hall. In the center of the picture, almost in Diana's lap, one sees a little dog. This is in fact *Biche*, leaning with her front paws on the thigh of the goddess of the hunt (clothed only in a towel), and gazing into the face of the beautiful one. [65] To Diana, virgin goddess of Roman mythology, mistress of wild animals, the forest and the hunt, were attributed healing powers, but also the power of death and ruination. Terrible in her anger, she is supposed to have demanded human sacrifice,

The Italian greyhound *Biche* (fr.: doe) in Diana's lap. For his art gallery Frederick also acquired the work *The Crowning of Diana* by Peter Paul Rubens, in which a large hunting dog leans on the goddess's thigh.

While playing the flute, Frederick would gaze at the painting *Diana with her Nymphs in the Bath*, painted by Antoine Pesne in 1747.

but by the same token protected those unjustly persecuted. She was also regarded as the preserver of innocence. From these qualities of Diana in combination with the traits of the highly sensitive *Biche*, one may also draw parallels to the personality of Frederick the Great, which was stamped by great sensitivity and emotional vulnerability, as well as by demanding, uncompromising coldness.

Regardless of whether the King, as sponsor of this mythological work, intended to establish a deep affinity between Diana, *Biche* and himself, the painting itself took on a unique significance through its grandeur alone, not to mention its prominent location in the music hall of the palace. In the thematically kindred painting by Adolph Menzel done more than a hundred years later, *The Flute Concert in Sanssouci*, Frederick's music stand is arranged in such a way that his gaze, as he plays the flute, falls on the goddess who holds his favorite dog *Biche* in her lap.

In the spring of 1747, two years after the cornerstone ceremony, the King intended to move into Sanssouci palace, which had been built according to his specifications and was to become his favorite residence. Totally unexpectedly, on February 13, at a mere 35 years of age, he suffered something of a mild stroke, from which he recovered only very slowly. In a letter dated March 11, he wrote to his brother August William:

*At times I feel almost healthy, but then those cramps come again, intermittently, which cause me great misery. Only exercise, diet and my constitution will, hopefully, make me whole again. If not, I'll be going to that land ... where I'll find Keyserlingk, Jordan and Borcke, where we'll stroll on Lethe's banks under evergreen trees and where all inhabitants of the earth finally arrive.*[66]

But Lethe, the mythical river of oblivion, would have to wait almost another forty years for him. For now, the King moved into the palace, which was still under construction. He had conceived the *vigne*, his vineyard house, as, in many respects, *come à Reinsberg*, like in Rheinsberg – as a little hideaway, a place offering space to just a few intimates. In the case of extensive invitations of the early period, such as those to the house-warming festivities, most of the guests invited to Sanssouci had to stay in the Potsdam City Palace, because it was only there that they could be properly fed. On Tuesday, May 2, 1747, the Berlinische Nachrichten von Staats- und gelehrten Sachen reported: *Yesterday His Majesty the King took occupancy of His newly built, uncommonly lavish summer palace Sanssouci at Potsdam, dining there at noon at a table with 200 covers, following which toward evening a concert was given by the Royal Orchestra.*[67] Frederick had five guest rooms furnished in the west wing of his vineyard house. The sole circular room at the end of the palace, the structural counterpart to the library on the east side, was reserved for Count Rothenburg. On June 24 the King wrote to him from his new domicile: *Happy he who comes to rest through wisdom; experience leads to moderation. In the long run, ambition is nothing but the virtue of the fool; it is a leader that leads us astray and breaks our neck; it plunges us into an abyss that is overgrown with flowers. Live well! I wish you health and contentment and assure you that I am your loyal friend.*[68]

In Sanssouci the King set down in writing his experiences and lessons from the Silesian Wars and sent all of it to the by now almost twenty-six-year-old August William with the title, *Die Generalprinzipien des Krieges* (General Principles of War), to prepare him for his future duties as heir apparent. Grateful and still full of reverence, the latter wrote on June 21, 1748: *No gift could have made me happier than the book with which you have honored me. I regard it as a sign of your trust and acknowledge its value more than ever. With tireless enthusiasm I will try to imprint the principles and rules it contains on my memory.* [69]

In good spirits, Frederick answered on August 13: *Your friendship is my present happiness, and if I should remain alive, it will be the consolation of my old age. Dear brother, always keep this same disposition towards me and be convinced that I absolutely reciprocate it.* [70]

Given such affection, it is not surprising that, the following year, the King, in that way unique to him, intended to entrust none other than Prince August William with an unusual office. The heir apparent was to stand godfather to his dog *Biche*, who was once again blessed with the joy of motherhood. Frederick had a letter – printed, crowned with turtledoves and transferring godparenthood – delivered to him in *Biche*'s name by his youngest brother Ferdinand:

*Most illustrious Prince*
*Most gracious Prince and Lord*
*Gracious Godfather.*
*Notwithstanding His Majesty's many warnings and suggestions for preserving my chastity, it has nevertheless*

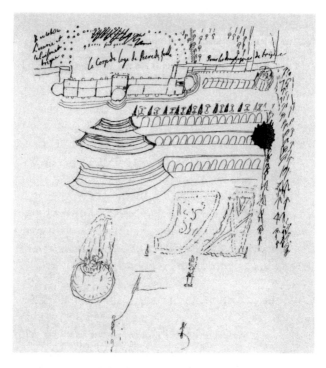

Lost drawing made by the King in his own hand of the ground plan and the terrace complex of Sanssouci.

*finally come to pass that I, through my dissolute, lustful life, have been made pregnant through the persuasion of two witnesses, Misters Alexander and Kienast, likewise also through the favors of the dog Mylord, and, moreover, that I, as of this date, have brought into the world comely canine children of my own species. Now since I, as an honorable canine mother, have resolved to give my beautiful young children their names next … , and since, particularly on such an occasion, the required witnesses and relatives are indispensible, therefore my most humble, amicable conduct is [hereby] submitted to Your Royal Highness as my most valued senior godfather, so that he may take upon himself this highly important task, and appear on the appointed day at … o'clock at the residence of my foster father, Mr. Theodor Kienast, and be present at this procedure with all due respect; and, at the conclusion of this most important task, my most honorable senior godfather will deign to take pleasure in a doggy soup beautifully prepared by my canine chef, along with an old, beautiful, well preserved bone, plus a bit of honeycomb and sugar. Above and beyond such favors and for as long as I shall live, I remain Your Royal Highness's most loyal, subservient Bigé,*

*Potsdam,*
*From my childbed*
*May, 1749.*[71]

August William answered his brother on May 27, 1749: *Ferdinand delivered the letter to me in which Biche invites me to stand godfather to her young. I am happy to accept this offer. I will not venture to say, He who loves the master will also love his dog, lest I imitate Sancho Panza, who spoke in proverbs. In any case, you can well imagine that I consider it an honor to be Biche's godfather.*

# Allerdurchlauchtigster Printz
# Gnädigster Printz und Herr
# Gnädiger Herr Gevatter.

Ohnerachtet derer vielen Warnungen und Vorstellungen meine Keuschheit zu erhalten, ist es doch endlich durch mein liederliches wollüstiges Leben dahin gekommen, daß ich durch Zureden zweyer Zeugen als des Herrn Alexander, und Kienast, ingleichen auch durch die Annehmlichkeit des Hundes Mylord bin geschwängert worden, auch heute dato wohlgestalte Hunde-Kinder meines Geschlechtes zur Welt gebracht. Da ich nun als eine Ehrliebende Hunde-Mutter resolviret meine unmündige schöne Kinder künftigen ihre Nahmen beyzulegen, und dabey absonderlich die nöthige Zeugen und Gevattern unentbehrlich seyn, so ergehet mein unterthänigstes freundlich Thun an Ewr. Königl. Hoheit als meines werthesten Herrn Gevatters dieses so wichtige Werck über sich zu nehmen, und ermeldten Tages um Uhr auf meines Pflege-Vaters Herrn Theodor Kienast Cammer zu erscheinen und diesem Actui mit aller Ehrbarkeit beywohnen, und nach Endigung dieses so wichtigen Werckes wollen sich Hochgeehrtester Herr Gevatter mit einer von meinem Hunde-Koche wohl zugerichteten Hunde Suppe, und einen alten schon lange aufgehobenen schönen Knochen, und ein bißgen Wachs und Zucker sich erfreuen. Vor alle diese Gnade werde ich so lange ich lebe seyn

## Ew. Königl. Hoheit

Potsdam,
aus meinem Wochen-Bette
den    May 1749.

unterthänigste treue
Bigé.

Gevatterbrief des Windspiels Biche für Prinz August Wilhelm (Faksimile).

144

*Loyalty and devotion, so rare among human beings, are almost universal among her kind, to the shame of those who do not possess these qualities. Surely there is nothing in the world from which a good moral may not be drawn! Biche alone would provide material for several volumes. May her progeny all inherit her good qualities, and may she herself, having successfully come through her confinement, continue to give you proofs of her loyalty. Having now sung Biche's praise, there remains nothing further for me to say.* [72]

The friendly words notwithstanding, Frederick could no longer ignore the fact that his brother's loyalty and devotion had shifted over time from him to their next-younger brother Henry. In various quarrels he had with the princes over their alleged poor military leadership, but also concerning his own policies towards the Russians, who were becoming increasingly aggressive in Europe, he had, to his great disappointment, to suffer seeing August William take sides with the twenty-three-year-old Henry. Added to this, he was in an extremely tense state of mind from a painful attack of gout in his legs. Possibly he now regretted his near-childish correspondence with the heir to the throne, particularly the letter adorned with turtle-doves. On May 29 he wrote to him quite unexpectedly: *Please excuse Biche's presumptuousness in asking you to be her godfather. There is nothing more cynical than dogs. So it is good of you to refrain from anger over her insolence.* [73]

# VI
*I see nothing but my pain.*
The Death of Count Rothenburg and of the Dog *Biche*
(1751-52)

It is well known that *Biche* was a gift to the King from
his close friend Rothenburg. The count's health had
been seriously compromised by his severe war injuries and due to his not especially healthy lifestyle. Yet
Rothenburg also extended himself to support Frederick II in realizing his peacetime projects. One of
these was the construction of St. Hedwig's Cathedral
in Berlin to which he contributed. Ignoring the reality of the sharply segregated religious communities,
Frederick had originally conceived this house of worship as a kind of pantheon of religious tolerance for
the most diverse persuasions but had felt compelled
to let himself be persuaded of the infeasibility of such
a project and finally agreed to the cathedral's exclu-
sive use by the Catholic Church. As chairman of the
advisory board and director of construction, Count
Rothenburg, himself a Catholic, was entrusted with
the management of building capital and the imple-
mentation of construction designs. In 1750 he convinced the King to turn the church, which for lack of
funds was going up only in fits and starts, over to the
financially powerful Roman order of Dominicans. By
now Rothenburg was already seriously ill. Concerned,
Frederick wrote him on April 8, 1750: *You would be
wise not to schedule your first venturing outside too early.*

*I'm well aware how tiresome it is to stay in your room for so long. But one also regrets it sometimes when one exposes oneself to the air too early, and with your lower back pain you must avoid the rattling of the coach. I embrace you. ... Be well.*[74]

Despite his almost undaunted *joie de vivre*, the headstrong patient's state of health declined steadily. Again the King turned to him with reprimand: *July 17, 1751. What's this! My dear Count, songs instead of medical advice! ... But I think it would be good to pay a little attention to your doctor's counsel. If I may venture my own opinion, I would combine the cure Cothenius advises with the diet La Mettrie suggests. I'll send you the notes and let me add that in your place I would not delay a single moment to use them as a guide. Eller and Cothenius are of the same opinion. The whole business will be a bit of a bother to you, but it is better to force oneself and live than to crawl into some dark grave, where one winds up soon enough anyway.*[75]

The political and personal importance that the count came to have for the King was enormous. Prince August William wrote his brother in September of 1751: *I was worried about you over the loss of Rothenburg. He was doing very badly and the doctors had almost run out of Latin. At the moment he is out of danger, barring a relapse. I was with him when he was doing quite poorly. He was a pathetic sight, but even in the most severe pain his spirit never lost its good cheer. In that kind of situation that is an added benefit; for it is the only way to suffer patiently and soothe the pain of the onlookers.*[76]

Three months later, on December 29, 1751, Count Rothenburg died at the young age of forty-one. On the following day Frederick turned to Wilhelmine: *Dearest sister! You, who have such a tender heart, have pity on my situation! ... yesterday Rothenburg passed away in my arms. I am unable to answer your letter; I see nothing but my pain. All my thoughts are riveted on the loss of a friend with whom I have lived in closest friendship for twelve years.*[77]

She answered: *Your last letter moved me profoundly. I could not hold back the tears when I read of the grief the death of Count Rothenburg caused you. I can easily put myself in your place, knowing as I do how rare good friends are on this earth and how hard it is to lose them. The very thought of the loss of a loved one makes the heart shudder. ... I swoon in mortal fear over your precious health. I know how deeply you feel, but that can only hurt you with your ailing health. With energy one can perhaps hide one's emotional life, but one's distress is not thereby banished. And so such energy is all the more dangerous since one is bottling up one's sorrow. The body is forced to suffer a double burden. ... I assure you, dearest brother, my thoughts do not leave you for a moment. Your condition causes me a pain that has left me quite dejected. I see you cooped up in your room, gloomy and lost in thought. God, how I worry about you!*[78]

The death of his friend left Frederick deeply shaken. He now drew up a will, which he put on file a scant two weeks after Rothenburg's death, thus January 11, 1752, just before his own 40th birthday.[79] In it he made clear that he was to be buried, not with the pomp and splendor of a ruler, but rather like a philosopher, in a modest grave, next to his dogs. His private will reads as follows: *Our life passes by in a flash. It speeds along, dragging us from birth to death. If I have made it my guiding principle to work with the greatest fervor on keeping the state, which I have had the honor to rule, in good order, if I, according to my best judgment and my best knowledge, have all my life done everything in my power to bring it to fruition, I would still reproach myself eternally if I neglected to record my last will and testament, thereby giving rise to all possible disputes and domestic quarrels that might break out after my death. These considerations have moved me to declare my last will in this solemn document. … Gladly do I give back my life's breath to beneficent nature, which has kindly granted it to me, and my body to the elements from which it is made. I have lived as a philosopher and wish to be buried as one, without pomp, without pageantry and without a trace of ceremony. I wish neither an open casket nor to be embalmed. If I die in Berlin or Potsdam, I do not wish to be put on display for the frivolous curiosity of the people and then be entombed on the third day at midnight. Let me, by the light of a lantern and with no one following, be brought to Sanssouci, there to be buried quite simply at the top of the terrace on the right side as one ascends it, in a grave I have arranged for myself.* [80]

Three days later, on January 14, 1752, he wrote to his sister in Bayreuth: *If anything has the power to console me, it would be your sympathy for my sad state. Quite frankly, I completely share your opinion that it doesn't pay to have deep regrets about one's life. What is life anyway when one loses all the people one spent the most time with, when death robs us forever of those we loved? I will tell you personally, the foolish figure I play fills me with revulsion; for me the world is totally vapid. ... In the first days I was in despair. I was able to assuage this first stirring of my spirit, but there remains in my soul a residual melancholy that I – and this I feel clearly – cannot so quickly wipe out. The tiniest memory strikes my heart like a dagger thrust. I believe only those are happy on earth who love no one. I seek to assuage my pain with the reading of Lucretius' third canto, but that gives back to me nothing of what is irretrievably gone. I work a good deal, to distract myself, and find that work provides the greatest relief. Don't worry about me, dear sister, I am not good enough to die soon, and take care of yourself lest you intensify my sorrow beyond measure.* [81]

Following Etienne Jordan and Dietrich von Keyserlingk, the king lost another close friend with the death of Count Rothenburg. One year after Rothenburg's death to the day, the dog *Biche* died. In his sorrow Frederick turned once again to Wilhelmine:

*(Berlin) 29 (December 1752)*

*Dearest sister! ... I have a domestic sorrow that has tossed my whole philosophy onto the trash heap. I confess to you my entire infirmity. I have lost Biche; her death has reawakened in me the memory of the loss of all my friends, especially the one who gave her to me. I was ashamed that the death of a dog could affect me so deeply, but the domestic life I lead and the loyalty of this poor animal caused it to grow very dear to my heart. Her suffering so moved me that I am now depressed and sad, to tell the truth. Should one be hard? Should one be without feeling? I believe that anyone who can be indifferent to a loyal animal will not be any more grateful to his peers, and that when one is faced with the choice, it is better to be too soft than too hard.*[82]

Wilhelmine answered with empathy: *Why do you call sorrow over Biche's death a weakness? In truth, the vulgar label "weakness" covers many sentiments which reason identifies as virtues. Is it remarkable that you loved an animal (that perhaps had the mere form of one) that was loyal, grateful and always ready to entertain you and read everything from your eyes? Such qualities are admirable among humans, but so rare that one can scarcely find a single one among thousands who possesses it and is a true friend. Folichon's death would cause me very great sorrow. He is a true companion to me in my loneliness, as Biche is to you. In her you had a friend who never caused you the slightest concern, being rather at pains to distract you for a while with her caresses and antics.*

*So is it really so surprising that you grieve over her? No, dear brother! A tender, sympathetic, devoted heart is never a weakness. You have such a heart. ... It seems fate is persecuting you by robbing you of your friends.*[83]

Frederick answered: *All your letters double my love for you; only a true friend could write letters like the last one I received from you. You take part in my petty concerns, you probe them and have sympathy for my sensitivity. I know it only concerns a dog, but everything you write to me about Folichon applies to Biche too, literally. Heaven has given us the same heart and the same feeling.*[84]

*Biche* was buried in the crypt at Sanssouci, in the spot the King had selected for his own demise after Rothenburg's death. Paulig reported: *"If one of the dogs died, a coffin would be made for him and set up in the King's library, before being buried in the grave on the terrace. The gravesite would then receive a plaque."*[85] The gravesite was a permanent reference to the inescapability of death. It was the spot on which the King gazed every day. The publisher Christoph Friedrich Nicolai wrote in his *Anekdoten von König Friedrich II. von Preußen* (Anecdotes about King Frederick II of Prussia) in the year 1789: *Already by the year 1744, just as the terraces were being laid out and even before the foundation of the palace was laid, the King had a crypt quietly dug on the open site just opposite the window of his study, in front of a semi-archway, and had the cove decked in marble and afterward a column of*

Even before beginning construction of the palace, the King had his gravesite laid out in the vineyard. The painting, by Johann Christoph Frisch (1780), in which Frederick the Great, accompanied by d'Argens, inspects the emerging gravesite in Sanssouci Park, was not made until after the death of the marquis, who was a great sponsor of the painter.

*flora laid on top of it. … It was in this crypt that the King wished to be buried. This crypt, the existence of which so few people knew, was probably the real reason for naming this place Sanssouci. The King had not yet given the house this name as it was being built. He called it his summerhouse, his vineyard summerhouse. Once, while walking on the site with d'Argens at the beginning of the palace's construction, he said to him: Since he had made the decision to build himself a summer residence in this pleasant spot, the idea simultaneously came to him to locate his grave in that very patch. "Quand je serai là," he said, pointing at the hidden grave, "je serai sans souci!"* [86]

Unlike in Rheinsberg, which the King had also called *mein Sanssouci,* here the name stood, not for the hope of a worry-free life in a new refuge, but for carefree times after death. As the first servant of his state, who had written to his sister only twelve days after coming to power, *henceforth the highest goddess is duty,* and, moreover, as a man tested by suffering, Frederick had come to take a detached view of his own existence. When he made that remark in d'Argens's presence, he had the terrible experience of the First Silesian War behind him, and the next war was imminent. One may assume that he no longer expected tranquility and concord in this world. *With the reading of Lucretius' third canto,* he had written to his sister on the occasion of his *Biche*'s death, *I seek to assuage my pain.* For the Roman poet too, freedom from care referred to the afterlife:

*It will be as if you had fallen asleep in death and were released from all dismal pain for the rest of time.*[87]

Frederick's turning away from the idea of earthly happiness, from the rising sun in the Rheinsberg concert hall, was the withdrawal of his wounded soul to more reliable things. Life had sorely tested this man who yearned deeply for friendship. Love and friendship for men or women could, in the end, only lead to despair or at least disillusionment; to this too the Roman poet Lucretius had attested. And so he channeled his passion more and more into work, the muses and especially his loyal Italian greyhounds. His contemporary Anton Friederich Büsching commented in hindsight in 1788: *Dogs were enormously important to Him, and he always had three or four of them around him, one of which would be His favorite, and the others the favorite's companions. All day long the former always lay near where the King sat, right beside him, on a special chair covered with two pillows, and at night slept in bed with Him. In the evening the others would be taken away; then the following morning, when He was awakened, they would be brought back, since the little circle amused the King with their hearty cheerfulness and affection. They sat next to Him on the sofas, which as a result became filthy and tattered, and the King allowed them everything. He looked after their maintenance, health and feeding most tenderly; even at table his favorite received something from the King's hand; in general, however, the dogs were cared for by a servant who in good weather took them out for an after-dinner walk after their meal so they could enjoy the fresh air. Any servant who stepped on a dog's paw out of careless-ness rarely avoided the King's wrath.*[88]

For Frederick his Italian greyhounds were spiritually kindred creatures, perhaps even endowed with reason. In his day this attitude was anything but self-evident. It was not until the general spread of Enlightenment ideas, which, among other things, came to grips with the dignity of the creature, that the relationship between man and animal would change, to some extent at least, in favor of the latter. That dogs could be more than mere objects of use for house, yard or hunt had already been established centuries earlier by Francis of Assisi and the Benedictine nun Hildegard of Bingen. In the 12th century she commented in her *Naturkunde* (Natu-ral History): *The dog ... has in its nature and its habits something of man. That is why it feels and knows people, loves them, stays by their side and is loyal to them. The devil hates dogs because of their loyalty to man and recoils from them. A dog recognizes hatred, anger and dishonesty in man and often growls over it. And when it knows that hatred or anger dominates a household, it grinds its teeth, "grumbles" with its teeth and mutters. Even when someone plans a betrayal, it snarls at him. ... Man's joy and sadness too it feels in advance. When something joyful is pending, it wags its tail happily; when something sad is pending, it howls sadly.*[89]

Even though Frederick would have agreed with these sentiments in principle, still it would not have been his way to take critical issue with the works of a nun. It was well known that he was not a religious man, rather rejecting the existing religious communities, which he nevertheless wished to see tolerated. He wrote to his sister: *And yet all these different confessions have just as many different doctrines, and each one swears to God that its own is the best. If an uneducated man, who knew nothing of* religion, *should hear these different fanatics disputing with one another, he would never be able to decide which one of them was right. Each of these religions, condemned by all the others, promises him salvation.*[90]

Still, in the final analysis, even Frederick believed in the existence of a God. Once from Rheinsberg he had shared his thoughts with Wilhelmine about a possible Creator: *The world and the rational beings inhabiting it are finite and have also had a beginning. But then there must be a supreme being to whom they owe their existence; for they cannot have arisen out of themselves since creative power is lacking to matter. This supreme being must be powerful because it has created them, wise because it has brought all things into a definite order, infinite because it encompasses so much being in its plan at once and because it was there before anything else was there. Therefore there is a Creator, and since this Creator is eternal and necessarily possesses all perfection, we, as His creatures, must worship Him, and He must be our God. ... Is not our origin more sublime if its Author is the epitome of all perfection; and is not the family tree of the world, so to speak, the more beautiful if it stems from so noble a root as a God would make: eternal, all-powerful, forbearing, indulgent, compassionate and gracious! I am so convinced of this teaching that I regard any doubt of its veracity as impossible.*[91]

This meditation on the creation also embraced animals as beings created by God and *blessed with reason* and was therefore attuned to the ideals of the Enlightenment, which encouraged a critical appreciation of man's humane interaction with the world's exploited and harassed creatures. The King himself showed interest in this topic: *When someone read an article to him about animal souls, he said to the mutt sitting on his lap, 'Hear that? It's talking about you. It says you have no spirit. But you do have spirit.*[92]

This question as to the nature of animals had been popularized a century earlier by the philosopher and natural scientist René Descartes. In his *Discours de la Méthode* (1637), he espoused the view that animals were nothing more than machines, which, to be sure, came *from the hands of God,* but, having not a jot of reason, functioned in the end no differently than a watch.[93] Predictably, this theory of the soulless animal machine, denied all sensitivity, even to pain, found legions of supporters, justifying as it did hunting, animal experiments, slaughter, abuse and any predatory interaction with a creature. A contemporary reports: *One thought nothing of beating a dog. One beat him with a stick with total indifference and laughed at those who felt sorry for animals, as though they could feel pain.*[94] The Cartesian automaton theory, however, also aroused spirited opposition. The renowned polymath Pierre-Louis Moreau de Maupertuis, whom the King as president of the Royal Academy of Sciences had called to Berlin in 1746 and who was himself a respected breeder of imposing Icelandic dogs, sketched in his creation theory a picture of sentient beings, *capables de sentiment.*[95] This appraisal was in accord with what Frederick had experienced over the years with his highly sensitive canine companions and especially with his favorite dog that had died in December of 1752.

For Franz Kugler's *Geschichte Friedrichs des Großen*, Adolph Menzel made four hundred ink drawings as models for woodcuts. Here *The King's Free Hour in Sanssouci* from 1868.

# VII

*Health is Better Than All the Treasures of the World.*
Worry over Wilhelmine and Fredersdorf, over
Folichon and Alkmene (1753-1755)

Six months after *Biche's* death, Fredersdorf's health
also deteriorated. Like Rothenburg before him, the
King's *factotum* also showed himself to be not especially receptive to medical advice, preferring to
try out his own remedies. Moreover, he carried on
a senseless dalliance with methods for making gold.
The following letter from 1753 expresses Frederick's
displeasure with this and shows as well his continuing grief over *Biche's* death, for which he laid total
blame on the doctors. The result was that he allowed
no doctors to treat *Biche's* similarly sickly successor
*Alkmene*, nicknamed *mene*. Rather he hoped for her
recovery through a whey cure *(petit lät)*.

*Thank you for the nice things you sent; I'll send every-
thing back to you. Health is better than all the treasures of the world. First take care that you get better;
then we can make gold and silver. And if you want to
practice quackery, better to experiment with gold and
silver than to put all sorts of blasted medicines into
your body! It's no joking matter; once you're dead, no-
body will come by to wake you up. My poor Biche has
to remain dead because 10 doctors cured her to death;
mene will take nothing but petit lät, and no dog-doctor
will lay a hand on her!* [96]

Fredersdorf's health continued to decline. However, by year's end a possibility for change presented itself, a change based on which Frederick could hope for an improvement at least in the sick man's external situation. His *factotum* made plans for a marriage with the well-to-do merchant's daughter, Karoline Marie Elisabeth Daum. The King viewed this union primarily as an aspect of patient care and encouraged Fredersdorf in his decision: *Better to get married today than tomorrow if it will help in your care.*[97] Fredersdorf wed on December 30, 1753, and lived from then on with his wife on the Zernikow estate near Rheinsberg. Through the gift of the estate Frederick was effectively making his friend the owner of a knight's manor, an unusual distinction, since ordinarily the King strictly forbade the transfer of knightly manors to commoners.

With this marriage life became even lonelier for Frederick. *Our social life has gone to hell,* the King declared in 1754 in a letter to his former reader, Claude Etienne Darget, who had withdrawn from the King's circle following the arrival of Voltaire in July, 1750, and finally returned to France in August, 1753, *the fool Voltaire is in Switzerland, the Italian Algarotti makes himself invisible, Maupertuis is lying in his sickbed, and d'Argens has injured his little finger and has his entire arm in a bandage, as though he'd been hit by a cannonball. I live with my books and will soon know people just as little as Jordan knows the streets of Berlin.*[98]

In Sanssouci, too, in the beginning, Frederick had gathered around himself a circle of leading figures. Over the years, however, in contrast to Rheinsberg, he judged this society much more critically. The eloquent philosophers of the Round Table had all too frequently shown themselves to be unequal to the real challenges of life. This sobering experience was one the King had had to endure with Baron von Keyserlingk and Etienne Jordan during the First Silesian War and again during the Seven Years' War with the Marquis d'Argens and Maupertuis. Still, for an amazingly long time and with mildly ironic sympathy he showed an interest in the various mundane concerns of his friends. But the more deeply he became shaped by wartime experience and grief and the more intensely he was challenged by life, the less able he was to take pleasure in the beautiful décor and the mannered rococo atmosphere of his surroundings. The more sharply he believed he could perceive the duplicity of those around him, the more he turned to the unduplicitous, his Italian greyhounds. These he could believe, on these he could rely. The dogs needed no extravagant pleasures; like him, they took joy in simple things. Once when the elderly but exceedingly fun-loving chamberlain Karl Ludwig von Pöllnitz described his most recent [social] pleasures, Frederick did not have the feeling of having missed anything: *Poellnitz told me about all the ... gala events in Berlin. ... With all these beautiful descriptions, I struck myself as so countrified that, on my next appearance in Berlin, I'm thinking of taking on a dancing master and a young French marquis, just to pick up some social polish.*[99]

Meanwhile the King was leaning towards a smaller social circle. During the year 1754 the court page *Carel* especially cheered him up with his natural character. The reference here is almost certainly to the fourteen-year-old Carl Friedrich von Pirch, who soon thereafter became one of his eight personal pages. Frederick liked *Carel* because he enjoyed playing with *Alkmene* and because he *was dry behind the ears.*[100]

In February of 1755 he wrote to Fredersdorf: *Carel is now fast friends with mene; we call him "white mene" now and he is divinely courteous! If you were healthy, all things considered, I would be at ease! May God protect you, my dear Fredersdorf! And let me not hear any bad news concerning you tomorrow! That is my fondest wish. … Be especially careful of colds; I've well noted that they are most harmful to you. And eat only as much as your appetite allows! Once we're past March, I will indeed take heart! Meanwhile, however, I'll admit that, whenever I write you, I'm always afraid of getting a sad reply. Little black mene sends you greetings. And the white one, silly beast, delivers this to you.*[101]

Three months later, Wilhelmine, also seriously ill, and her husband, who had in the meanwhile separated from his mistress, not least due to Frederick's intervention, returned from an extended trip through France and Italy, a trip they had begun a year earlier, in hopes of aiding Wilhelmine's recovery with the warm climate and change of air. But the journey proved to be extremely grueling. The Margravine, wisely foresightful, had left her aging dwarf spaniel *Folichon* behind in Bayreuth. While in Rome she learned of the little dog's death and wrote to her brother: *May 20 – I must confess that I am very sad today. I just lost a loyal friend, one who delighted me in my leisure hours and was more devoted to me than any humans have ever been. My poor Folichon died in Bayreuth of old age. I had left him there, lest anything untoward happen to him on the trip, for he was no longer up to traveling. You know, dear brother, how deeply such small matters affect us, things most people just laugh about. It seems to me, however, when one gets to know people, one must withdraw from them, and we find much greater virtue among the so-called animals than among beings endowed with reason. I constantly see this reason become unreasonable and lead to evil. There are no genuine, loyal friends. The slightest advantage makes them forget all gratitude and friendship. It's often the one who seems most loving who becomes the most implacable foe.*[102]

In her memoirs, too, Wilhelmine recalled Folichon's death: *We finally departed two days later and returned to Erlangen. There I experienced a little domestic vexation. My Bolognese, whom I had had for nineteen years, died. I loved this little animal very dearly, having had it as a companion through all my sufferings, and his death grieved me deeply. Animals strike me as being rational beings, in their way; I've known some that were so smart that they lacked only language to express themselves clearly. In this respect I find Descartes's system quite ridiculous. I respect a dog's loyalty; in this it seems to have a value over humans, who are so fickle and changeable. If I were to pursue the matter in depth, I would at once be able to offer proof that greater reason prevails among animals than among men.*[103]

*Folichon* has been pictorially preserved for posterity many times over: in Wilhelmine's arm in the paintings of Antoine Pesne and Juda Löw Pinhas, in the drawings

A sketch by Adolph Menzel for the painting *Das Flötenkonzert Friedrichs II. in Sanssouci* (Frederick the II's Flute Concert in Sanssouci) of 1850, created one hundred years after the concert that was given on the occasion of the Margravine's visit to Potsdam. In the famous picture the delicate Wilhelmine also sits on a sofa, just behind her brother who is playing the flute.

of Adolph Menzel, in the ceiling fresco of Wilhelm Ernst Wunder in the Old Music Room of the New Palace in Bayreuth, as a Meissen porcelain figurine and as part of the previously mentioned marble statue in the Temple of Friendship in Sanssouci Park. And finally as a gravestone placed by Wilhelmine herself for her favorite dog.

The sadness over *Folichon* and serious concern for Frederick did not aid Wilhelmine's recovery – on the contrary. Following her return from the Italian journey, her health deteriorated markedly. Moreover, during her absence her brother's situation had become highly problematic due to growing political tensions. *All of Europe is in fermentation,"* he wrote to August William, *"our position is still not at all clear … Now we will see what, in the name of our security, is yet to happen or not happen.*[104]

At the beginning of 1756, the constellations of power among the European nations had changed considerably. England was primarily concerned with strengthening its colonial and naval power and therefore had only a mild interest in events on the continent. Thus it was of little help to Austria as a coalition partner. Consequently Maria Theresa sought support from France – alas, for quite a while this support was not forthcoming. France's standoffishness did not change until Louis XV learned that  Frederick II had agreed to a mutual defense pact with his archenemy England on January 16. Now readiness grew on the

French side to give up the alliance with Prussia. The Versailles treaty of May 1, 1756, sealed the Franco-Austrian alliance. The great anti-Prussian coalition was established.

One nation after another – first Russia under Czarina Elisabeth, then Poland and Saxony and finally even Sweden, where Frederick's sister Ulrike was the King's uninfluential consort – turned against Prussia through treaties and alliances. Three times Frederick had requested clarification from Maria Theresa concerning the buildup of troops in Bohemia and the alleged pact concluded with Russia against Prussia. The Austrian court dismissed the allegations as unfounded and false. But the Prussian King adhered to his appraisal, stating, *The Queen of Hungary had nothing in mind but the recovery of Silesia, which she had relinquished in two formal treaties. She mobilized all of Europe against us.*

Being far inferior to the opposing forces in terms of numbers, Frederick saw a preemptive strike as the only way out of the threat: *It was necessary to jump the gun so as not to be outdone.* On August 28, 1756, the King left Berlin and trekked with his troops through Saxony in the direction of Bohemia.

# VIII

*Never Before in Such Dire Straits*
The Misery of the Seven Years' War
(1756-1763)

With the march of Prussian troops into a totally unprepared Saxony, the so-called Seven Years' War began. With this hostile action Frederick provoked widespread outrage in Europe. Maria Theresa took advantage of this mood against Prussia and made pacts of aggression with those governments that heretofore had been bound to her by defense alliances alone. Following a few military successes in the first months, Frederick's situation became problematic over the year that followed; he had to endure great losses and even to retreat from Prague on June 18, 1757. On top of that, a report of the death of his mother reached him in the field. Queen Sophie Dorothea had died on June 28. On June 25, 1757, the chamberlain of Queen Elisabeth Christine, Ernst Ahasverus Count von Lehndorff, describes the atmosphere of a final dinner with the Queen Mother in Monbijou Palace, an atmosphere clouded by the events of war: *Our losses are great, primarily because of their consequences. Now we are again as far behind as we were after our entry into Bohemia, but with 30,000 fewer men, which the Battle of Reichenberg, the siege of Prague and the setback at Kolin have cost us. In the last battle, all our generals were either wounded or killed. ... Our enemies triumph to an absurd degree, and the newspapers are full of their vainglory. After dinner we experience a funny adventure. Frau v. Brandt, who despite having reached a certain age, remains beautiful and extremely coquettish, … is sitting there at the table and all of a sudden senses a strange movement going on beneath her, which becomes more and more vigorous, causing her to scream out loud, even though she's sitting next to the Princess. Everybody gets up, and it turns out that two dogs had crept under her chair and there, while involved in a certain activity, had produced the movements that alternately raised and lowered Frau v. Brandt's chair. We laughed all the harder since the incident happened to a lady who was well acquainted with such movements.*

*June 28, 1757. The Queen Mother is dead! Only yesterday evening she dined with the young ladies v. Knesebeck and v. Bredow, trading quips with the latter.*[105]

The report of her death reached Frederick on July 2 in the Leitmeritz army camp in North Bohemia. The English special envoy, Sir Andrew Mitchell, who was accompanying the Prussian troops, noted: *The King went into seclusion in order to weep and grieve over this new harsh sorrow, which was added on to so many other afflictions. … For two days he held no morning receptions; only the Princes* (his brothers Heinrich and Ferdinand) *dined with him. … Yesterday, July 3, the King had me summoned in the afternoon – it was the first time he had received anyone since the report arrived – I had the honor of spending a few hours with him in his chambers. I must confess it affected me deeply to see him so caught up in his pain and giving himself up to the tenderest childlike feelings; he recalled the many obligations he had to Her Deceased Majesty, all that she had suffered and how nobly she bore it, how much kindness she had showed to everyone. His only consolation, he added, was the thought that he had striven to make her last years pleasant.*[106]

On July 5 Frederick wrote to the seriously ill Wilhelmine in Bayreuth: *A new sorrow to weigh upon us! We no longer have a mother. This loss puts the crown on my pain. I have to act and hardly have time to give my tears free run. You can imagine the condition of a feeling heart that is put to such a cruel test. All losses on earth can be put right, only those caused by death are irreplaceable. … I entreat heaven to keep you.*[107]

While Frederick mourned his mother, the French occupied Emden in the extreme west and the Russians Memel in the east. In close proximity to him, the Austrians were already gathering. On July 13 he again turned to his sister: *So many blows strike me that I am as though numbed. … I am firmly decided to make every effort to save my fatherland, regardless of whether Fortuna smiles upon me or completely turns her back to me. … I bless the hour when I became acquainted with philosophy. She alone can elevate the soul in a situation such as mine. I give you an extensive account of my trials, dear sister. If they affected me alone, my soul would not be oppressed; but I must watch over the wellbeing and woe of a people*

Prince August William, the designated heir to the throne with the Order of the Black Eagle, the family order of the Prussian royal house. Frederick the II's grandfather had established it in 1701 to celebrate the dignity of the royal house. In the medallion the Prussian eagle is depicted, framed by the motto *Suum cuique* (*To each his own*) (Antoine Pesne, 1753).

*that have been entrusted to me. That is the crux of the matter. I must reproach myself for the slightest error, if I, through either slowness or hastiness, become responsible for the slightest hitch, especially at the present time when all errors are capital errors.*[108]

In the face of the threat from 70,000 Austrian soldiers, the heir to the throne, Prince August William, was, unfortunately, far from up to fulfilling the expectations placed on him as a military commander. Frederick was beside himself with dismay over his dithering conduct and wrote to him on July 30, 1757: *Your bad behavior has shifted my affairs into a desperate situation. It is not my enemies who are ruining me but your poor course of action. My generals are without excuse; they have either advised you poorly or approved your poor decisions. Your ears are only used to the language of your sycophants; … There is no other choice left to me in this sad situation but to take quite desperate measures. I will fight, and, if we cannot prevail, we will all get ourselves killed. I do not accuse your heart but your ineptitude and your paltry power of judgment in your choice of decisions. I speak openly to you. He who has but a brief span of life left need keep no secrets. I wish you more good fortune than I have had. May you learn in time to come, after all the humiliating adventures that have befallen you, to deal with these great affairs more thoroughly, more judiciously and more decisively! The disaster I foresee is, in part, your fault. You and your children – you will be more severely punished for it than I will. Still, have no doubt that I have always loved you and that I will die with this feeling.*[109]

Against the express wishes of the King, who wanted him to continue serving in the army as a model of *steadfastness and honor*, August William retired to Berlin and, finally, to his palace in Oranienburg, deeply disappointed: *Dearest brother! Since you have once again reproached me for my shortcomings, I am so totally convinced of my unfitness and my uselessness for the army that I will probably have to guard against becoming a liability to you. Still, I cannot deny that it pains me deeply that all my effort and diligence were for naught and that I must see myself at my age as a useless member of the state. So I believe there is nothing left for me but to lead a secluded life.*[110]

During these dramatic events, Antoine Pesne died on August 5, almost unnoticed, in his Berlin house, Oberwallstraße 3. With forty-six years of activity as a painter at the Prussian court, he was long regarded as the most important artist in Berlin. His paintings afforded – then as now – the most authentic and, frequently, the only possibility of envisioning the three Prussian Kings and their environs. After seeing the portrait of his mother, Queen Sophie Dorothea, painted by Pesne in 1737, Frederick, brimming with inspiration, waxed poetic: *What brilliant spectacle that lives before my eyes! To godly heights, dear Pesne, your paintbrush lets you rise. … And so your art doth*

Pesne, born in Paris in 1683, entered the service of Frederick I in 1711. Upon assuming the government, Frederick Wilhelm I reduced his salary by half. In order to maintain his connection to the city of his birth, the painter applied to the Paris Academy with an outsized portrait of his family. He revered Watteau, who died in 1721, one year after Pesne's acceptance to the Academy (*The court painter Antoine Pesne* drawing based on a detail from the *Family Portrait* of 1718).

*work with wondrous strength as ever, Most any like-*
*ness imitates a sorcerer's endeavor. ... Dare anyone our*
*fair Queen's painted image render – For sure, a Pesne*
*may, but dabblers must surrender.*[111]

When the scolded Prince August William learned
of the death of the esteemed artist, he wrote his sister-
in-law, the wife of Prince Heinrich, *Poor Pesne is dead,*
*and the arts in Berlin are buried with him.*[112]

In the further course of the year 1757, even Berlin
itself was made to feel the repercussions of the war.
Maria Theresa's generals had adopted the plan to move
from Bohemia and Saxony to just before the gates of the
capital city. Count Lehndorff, who witnessed the devas-
tating impact of this undertaking at the court of Queen
Elisabeth Christine in Schönhausen Palace, recorded
in his diary under October 16, 1757: *The toughest, sad-*
*dest day of my life! No sooner had I got out of bed than*
*the word was: the enemy is at the gates. On all sides*
*one sees half-naked men speeding past,* fleeing from
the area. *At 8 o'clock the Queen summons me. I find*
*this worthy ruler in tears. She orders me to inform all*
*princesses that she will depart at 11 o'clock, in case they*
*wish to join her. When all are assembled, the Queen*
*says they must follow the King's command and leave.*
*... When we get to Spandau, the news is that Berlin has*
*been plundered and everyone's been massacred. Now*
*we no longer feel safe even in the city of Spandau, and*
*the entire royal house has to take lodging in the fortress.*
*The building in which so many noble figures are to find*

*accommodation has, since Frederick I, served only as a place to house prisoners and store ammunition. The Queen's arrival was not expected, so there is neither fire nor light on hand. Four criminals, irons on their feet and a small lamp in hand, show Her Majesty and the princesses into the quarters, which consist of five rooms in which the windows are broken, the doors don't lock, and not a chair is to be seen. October 21, 1757. His Majesty is not coming to Berlin but has drawn close to himself all regiments that had been deployed for our reassurance, and we are to go to Magdeburg.*[113]

In this seemingly hopeless situation, Frederick wrote to Wilhelmine: *You alone still fetter me to this world; my friends, my dearest relatives rest in their graves; in short, I have lost everything. Should you take the same decision as I, then together we will end our unhappiness and misfortune. Then may those who remain in the world take those tribulations upon themselves that are placed upon them and carry the burden that we have dragged for so long.*[114]

The otherwise exceedingly empathic sister showed little understanding for the idea of a mutual pact to end it all. She implored her brother to keep faith in his historical mission, comparing him to Caesar and Louis XIV, who prevailed in the end in the face of adversity. And once again Frederick succeeded in overcoming his inner abyss and improving his military situation. However, following an unexpected Prussian victory at

Rossbach in early November, only two weeks later the tide turned again. Count Lehndorff noted in his diary, *It is said the King was cut to the quick by the horrible report. Schweidnitz, Liegnitz and just generally a large section of Silesia is in enemy hands.*[115]

At this time Frederick composed another decree for the instance of his death. In the Disposition of November 21, 1757, as to *what should take place if I am killed,"* he again specified: *"As for the rest, concerning my person, I wish to be laid to rest at Sanssouci, without ostentation, without pomp and at night. My body is not to be displayed, but is to be brought there without fuss and buried at night.*[116]

In this desolate state of armed conflict, the King longed for distraction, for philosophical discussion and fine art, for all the pursuits he himself called his intellectual *medicine.* He asked the Marquis d'Argens to keep him company in Breslau. Jean-Baptiste de Boyer Marquis d'Argens, an enlightened French philosopher, whose writings Frederick had treasured since his days as Crown Prince, had entered the King's service as chamberlain in 1742. To be sure, it required some considerable persuasion to entice the Marquis to Silesia. Frederick wrote in December of 1757: *Truly, you would be performing a good work if you came for a visit. I am without company and without support. ... I'll send someone to accompany you and cover the cost of horses and all expenses. So now, dear Marquis, fresh courage! We will seal off every draft; I'll provide woolens, furs and hoods to bundle you up in. You'll view Bernini's beautiful mausoleum in the cathedral, … Feel free to bring your wife with you.*[117] At the end of the year, the Marquis finally arrived in Breslau, wrapped in furs and equipped with hot-water bags, medicine chests, etc., and, at any rate, remained at the King's side for three months, the King dining and conversing with him. Shortly before the Marquis's trip home, the very natural-mannered Henri de Catt, from Switzerland, had entered the King's service as royal reader. In his notes he reported that, even during campaigns, Frederick would seek conversation for an hour or two in the afternoon, or play the flute or compose or that he would recite such tragedies as Andromaque, Phèdre, Brittanicus, Mithridate or Athalie with deep inner empathy.

In the end it was intellectual and musical activities that helped the King to numb his pain and worry. He confessed to his youngest sister, Amalie, herself a devoted performer and composer of music, that it was especially when he composed verse – he called it *Verseschmieden* (literally: verse-forging) – that he felt great distraction from his unhappiness. It was the same for him with stimulating reading. To divert his mind from negative thoughts, he is said to have read, with minimal interruptions, the sixteen-volume world history of the French historian Jaques-Auguste de Thou and the thirty-six-volume church history of the French cleric Claude Fleury.

On January 12, 1758, while the Marquis d'Argens was still residing in Breslau, Michael Gabriel Fredersdorf died on his Zernikow estate in Brandenburg. The historian Johannes Richter remarked on the premature death of the forty-nine-year-old man, *The great commotion, the ups and downs of mood during the war year 1757, may have contributed to robbing him of his last powers.*[118] *Fredersdorf had stood by Frederick's side for almost thirty years and carved out an incredible career for his era. Count Lehndorff noted in his diary on October 23, 1757, just three months before Fredersdorf's death:*

*I then paid another visit to the famous Fredersdorf, who under the title of King's chamberlain played for so long the role of a prime minister. Basically this man exercised every office of the court. He supervised all construction projects as well as the King's finances; all domestic workers depended on him; in short, after the King he was the only one who ruled, and that often quite despotically. These days he is ailing; his hemorrhoids have almost eaten him up. And yet how astonishing that a most common man without the slightest education from the farthest reaches of Pomerania has been able to acquire such propriety, intellect and manners. A quite handsome face did advance his cause, providing the beginning of his good fortune.*[119]

The personal losses, which the King was compelled to experience along with all the chaos of war, did not end with Fredersdorf's death, to say the least. He had also long since had his own slow passing before his mind's eye. Henri de Catt noted on June 10, 1758, during the encampment in Moravia: *At five o'clock I found the King busy drawing Sanssouci Palace, the gardens, the colonnade, the little Chinese palace, on paper, all of which he had sketched for me once before. "Here, have a look at the beautiful project I'm planning!" Noticing a kind of mausoleum at the end of the terrace near a little grove, I asked him whether it was an antique structure of some sort. "No, my dear fellow, it's a crypt. I'll have cypresses planted all around it, and there will be my final resting place. Don't you agree that I'll be well protected there?" "Your Majesty is expressing a sad thought." "How so? Do we not have to die some day, and should we not give thought to this end? Indeed, should we not think about it in all calm, and should not I do this more than anyone else?*[120]

As prepared as the King was to accept his own death, the thought of taking leave of his intimates was as painful and difficult to him then as before. Two days after de Catt's diary entry, the heir to the throne Prince August William died in Oranienburg Palace at the age of thirty-five. Doctors cited a bad fall from his horse as a contributory cause of the Crown Prince's death, a fall he had suffered in 1744 during the siege of Prague. But his conflict with the King may also have broken his will to live, since Prince August William had refused proper medical treatment. Upon receiving the death announcement, Frederick took a long, lonely ride.[121]

The eldest son of the decedent, the by-then thirteen-year-old Frederick William, was now the next pretender to the throne. From his army camp in the South Moravian town of Prossnitz, the King wrote, on June 21, 1758, to the elderly Field Marshal Christoph Wilhelm von Kalkstein, who had reared him for ten years from the age of six, to be sure, according to strict paternal standards, yet with great kindness and sympathy:

*My dear Field Marshal! A series of fateful blows that have pursued me for years has snatched a brother from me, a brother I loved dearly despite all the trouble he caused me. His death imposes on me the sad duty to take care of his children and take on the roll of father to them. Since I am far away and great tasks burden me, I cannot see to their upbringing. However, in view of the staunch allegiance you have already shown to my father and to the state, and considering your friendship with the deceased, which you, as I hope, also cherish for me, I implore you to keep an eye on the upbringing of those poor children. You know how significant it is for several million souls that they be brought up well.*

*Your loyal friend,*
*Frederick* [122]

Two months later, on August 22, 1758, three days before the battle against the Russian forces at Zorndorf, Frederick again gave orders to the generals as to *how they are to conduct themselves in case I should be shot dead.*

Once again he specified, *I am not to be displayed, rather I am to be quietly brought to Sanssouci and buried in my garden.*[123] Following the battle that numbered 13,000 dead on the Prussian and 18,000 (on Frederick's own assertion, as many as 30,000) on the Russian side, in which the King, deploying all his forces, eventually triumphed, neither the repercussions of the incredible slaughter nor the victory of his own troops really seemed to move him. Almost numbed by overextension, he mourned only the death of his aide-de-camp Karl Friedrich von Oppen and was concerned over the life of his gravely ill sister, of whose impending death he had a presentiment. On October 12, immediately before the next great battle, that of Hochkirch, against superior Austrian forces, his thoughts again turned to her, thoughts he put in an *Epistle: So many gods in the stream of time/ Did man create, … The only one to be a temple worth;/ The god of friendship no folk cares to birth./ …You sister, whom to goddess I did raise,/ Deeply honored one, whose brother I/ do proudly call myself … Your soothing word/ Has often freed me from all sorrow's spell./ O you my sole resort, my certain port!/ Your virtue's strength let me endure this orb./ So many dangers to absorb/ Your lofty sensibility so true,/ When I did long for death,/ Did hide from me sepulchral sorrow's view,/ … It's you we do build altars to!* [124]

Two days later Wilhelmine died at the age of forty-nine in Bayreuth. That same night of October 14, 1758,

Frederick lost the Battle of Hochkirch. The death of his beloved sister shook him far more than the military defeat. Yet, against expectations, the King did not give up this time either. He gathered new forces, had his brother Henry join him with an extra six thousand soldiers and, despite all the lethal blows of fate and defeats at year's end, managed – contrary to all Europe's expectations – to avoid annihilation. In fact, with the retreat of the Austrians, his position developed in an unexpected positive direction. Still, his mood remained pensive. On November 23 he wrote to Hereditary Marshal George Keith, the brother of his friend who had fallen at Hochkirch five weeks earlier: *There is nothing left for us to do, my dear Mylord, but mingle and unite our tears over the losses we have suffered. If my head were a fountain of tears, it would not be adequate to my pain. Our campaign is over and nothing has been accomplished on either side but the loss of many good men; the misfortune of many poor soldiers, crippled forever; the ruin of several provinces; the devastation, plundering and burning of a number of flourishing cities. Those, my dear Mylord, are facts to make men shudder; the sad consequences of the nefariousness and ambition of certain powerful people ready to sacrifice everything to their boundless passions! I wish you, my dear Mylord, nothing that resembles my fate in the slightest and everything lacking to it.* [125]

To the Marquis d'Argens, who in the meantime had secluded himself in the safe city of Hamburg, he wrote on December 22: *I have lost everything I loved*

*and valued on this earth; I am surrounded by unfor-*
*tunates whom I cannot stand by in the crisis of these*
*times. I am still completely crushed by the devastation*
*of our most beautiful provinces and by atrocities com-*
*mitted therein by a horde more animal then human.*
*Heading into old age, I have been demeaned almost to*
*the level of a theater king, and you will grant that such*
*a position is not sufficiently appealing to bind the soul*
*of a philosopher to life. … Eat oysters and lobster in*
*Hamburg, down all the pills from the pharmacies, use*
*all the enemas in the baths and lock yourself hermeti-*
*cally into your room; but while you're enjoying these*
*blessings like the elect in paradise, do not forget a poor*
*soul cursed by God, one condemned to fight a running*
*battle with life to the end of time and succumb to the*
*burden of his work.*[126]

Following a Prussian victory in the battle of Liegnitz
in August, 1760, he again confessed to the Marquis
d'Argens, *In my entire life I have never been in so bad a*
*situation as in this campaign. Believe me when I say it*
*will take a miracle to overcome all the difficulties I still*
*behold before me.*[127]

And a miracle it was. Leastwise it was not by means of
a military triumph but rather an entirely unexpected
event that hostilities took a turn that would ultimately
lead to peace. This turn announced itself in January,
1762, with the report of the death of the childless Russian Czarina, Elisabeth I. On December 25, 1761 – the
news not reaching Western Europe until mid-January

– Duke Karl Peter Ulrich von Holstein-Gottorp, ridiculed and despised within Russia, assumed the czar's throne in St. Petersberg. Friedrich Rudolf Paulig, biographer of the first four Prussian Kings, observed, *Her nephew and successor, Peter III, was an ardent admirer of the Prussian King. He carried Frederick's image in a ring on his finger. He was familiar with the King's campaigns and regarded Frederick as a paragon to be emulated.* [128] As an admirer of Frederick II, Grand Duke Peter had always regretted Russia's joining the anti-Prussian coalition; he felt himself to be a German and hated the Russian homeland that had been forced upon him. So it is no surprise that, following this transition of power in Petersburg, the Prussian King wrote to his budget minister, Finck von Finckenstein, *Can you see this first ray of light coming up for us! Praise heaven for it! We must hope that good weather will follow upon these storms. May God grant.* [129] On February 23, 1762 – much to the chagrin of Vienna – Peter III proclaimed a decree to all foreign Excellencies in Petersburg to the effect that *peace is to be concluded with the King of Prussia; that His Majesty the Czar for his own part is firmly decided on it; that he returns East Prussia and the so-called conquests that have been made and that Russia's participation in this war has ceased.* [130]

The peace and friendship treaty was signed on May 5, 1762, in St. Petersburg. On May 22, Sweden, a dependency of Russia, also agreed to an armistice. Bellicose skirmishes with Austria, however, continued apace, when on July 17 the totally unexpected report came in: *Revolution in Petersburg (July 9); Czar Peter, Your Majesty's admirer, is deposed; perhaps murdered.* [131]

Sophie Friederike Auguste, daughter of the Prince of Anhalt-Zerbst-Dornburg, who had been badly treated by her husband, the Czar, had herself declared *Catherine, Czarina of Russia*. She would go down in history as *Catherine the Great*. The Prussian King was extremely disturbed by this changed situation, but his concern proved to be unfounded. As Friedrich Rudolf Paulig observed: *The worst of Frederick's fears, a new alliance of Russia with his enemies, did not occur. Catherine believed Frederick to be the disturber of her marital peace. But when she sifted through her husband's correspondence after his murder, she discovered that Frederick had not slandered, but rather defended, her, that he had not spoken of her with ridicule but in a conciliatory way. Frederick had requested of Peter that he treat her, if not with affection, then at least with respect before the world. The Empress was moved to tears by this. She then announced that she would uphold the peace agreement.*[132]

It is doubtful that the King's delicacy of feeling was the decisive factor in the renewed confirmation of peace. Above all, the treaty with Russia, which brought the end of the Seven Years' War to within close proximity, favored Catherine's internal consolidation of power. As early as July, 1762, the new Czarina concluded peace. Frederick wrote to the Marquis d'Argens on July 21,

*The peace I have concluded with Russia remains in effect, but the alliance has turned to water. All troops are marching back to Russia, and so I stand completely alone.*[133]

At this point the King was at least freed from the burden of simultaneous battles against the Russians and the Austrians. He could concentrate exclusively on the conflict with Austria. His next objective was to drive the enemy out of Schweidnitz, the last remaining stronghold of Maria Theresa's troops on Prussian soil. The fortress was finally taken on October 9, notwithstanding strong resistance. On October 29, Prince Henry, the King's second-youngest brother, defeated opposing forces in a decisive battle at Freiberg in Saxony. Now Frederick was hoping for a readiness for peace on the part of a profoundly weakened Austria, especially since a preliminary peace had already been signed between England and France on November 3.

After the victory at Freiberg, the King was drawn to the porcelain factory in Meissen, as in earlier years. He cherished porcelain and had, since coming to power, endeavored to establish a comparable factory in Prussia. Of course, the secret of producing porcelain, to which the Saxons were privy, would not be so easily ascertained. In the 1750's Wilhelm Caspar Wegely had already tried and failed to produce valuable porcelain in Berlin. Beginning in 1761, Johann Ernst Gotskowsky made another attempt to realize the King's dream.

As early as January, Frederick was able to examine the first pieces, the quality of which, however, quite obviously fell far below Saxon standards. There were still problems with the colors purple and red, thicker staining causing unwanted bubble formation. Moreover, the beautiful white foundation color of Meissen porcelain was far from being reproduced. After failing to woo away the renowned porcelain modeler Johann Joachim Kaendler from Meissen, the King commissioned him to make porcelain for the Prussian court, giving him very detailed specifications regarding form, color and décor – perhaps in this way ferreting out further little secrets of porcelain production. He also had a touching gift made for the by-now seventy-six-year-old Countess Camas, a gift he sent to her with friendly regards:

*Meissen, November 20, 1762*
*I send you, my dear little mother, a little memory of me. You can use this box for make-up or for beauty marks or for snuff tobacco or for chocolates or for pills. But however you use it, when you look at the dog painted on the lid, the symbol of loyalty, give at least a thought to the fact that the loyalty of its giver puts that of all dogs in the world in the shade and that his devotion to you has nothing in common with the fragile substance of which the lid consists.*[134]

Circumstances began to change in the King's favor in the most varied spheres. In October the merchant Gotzkowsky sought him out in his Saxon encampment

Dwarf spaniel after a model by Johann Joachim Kaendler, the originator of Meissen porcelain sculpture, ca. 1745

in order to present him with the latest porcelain, which in the meantime had been produced in Berlin with Saxon porcelain clay. The King's excitement was great; Prussia was now truly in a position, as the factory manager Johann Georg Grieninger declared (not without pride), to produce *the most beautiful milky white porcelain pieces.*[135] Also, in November of 1762, after seven years of the brutal ravages of war, Frederick ordered a coffee service displaying motifs of an untroubled world, with *blue Watteauesque figures.*

There were, finally, hopeful developments on the political front as well. Allies of both Austria and Prussia had by then bowed out of the war; the coffers were empty and Austria itself was defeated on many counts. At this point Empress Maria Theresa too wanted peace. On February 15, 1763, the relevant documents were signed at the Saxon hunting lodge Hubertusburg. Silesia, including the County of Glatz, would now at last remain a permanent Prussian possession, while Saxony, as one of the electorates of the Holy Roman Empire, was restituted without territorial losses.

After the Seven Years' War, Prussia was a major European power. Yet, upon being congratulated on the peace agreement and hearing it suggested that this must be the most beautiful day of his life, the King answered: *The most beautiful day in life is the one on which one leaves it.*[136]

From Hubertusburg the King travelled to Breslau and, subsequently, along the Oder. On the return journey, he put up, as Friedrich Rudolf Paulig tells it, *at Frankfurt, in order to revisit here the site of his greatest defeat, the battlefield at Kunersdorf. While he lingered there for several hours in painful remembrance of those who had found their deaths for him here, Berlin was immersed in joyful excitement.*[137]

During his years of absence, the King, by now fifty-one, had changed greatly. To Countess Camas, who was staying at Schönhausen Palace with Queen Elisabeth Christine, he wrote on March 6, 1763, from Dahlen: *So I will see you again, my best Mama, and I hope it will be toward the end of this month or the beginning of April, and that I find you just as well as when I left you. As for me, you'll find that I've grown old and almost chatty, and gray as a donkey. I lose a tooth every day and am half lame from gout.*[138]

On March 30 the King arrived in Berlin. Riding in an inconspicuous old coach, he chose a circuitous route in order to reach the palace under cover of darkness, unnoticed by the people. He had no desire to receive the tumultuous ovations of thousands of enthusiastic Berliners immediately following his return from Kunersdorf. The careworn King wrote to his sister Ulrike in Sweden, *"I find myself in a city where I recognize the walls but where I do not rediscover the people who were the objects of my respect or my friendship."* [139] Soon after his arrival, as Franz Kugler reported in his biography first published in 1841, Frederick is said to have gone to Charlottenburg and called musicians and singers to the palace with instructions to perform Graun's *Te Deum* in the chapel. The King then entered the palace chapel unaccompanied, sat down and gave the signal to begin. As the choral voices intoned the words of the hymn of praise, he rested his head on his hand and wept.

Frederick had always felt his friendships in great depth, to the point where they became for him the only source of his personal happiness. In the wake of his tragic experiences in war and the loss of those closest to him, he withdrew more and more, in order, as he put it to the Marquis d'Argens, *to calm myself … and, in silencing the passions, to reflect on myself, to collect myself in my innermost soul and distance myself from every representation, which, to tell the truth, becomes day by day more unbearable to me.* [140] His experience, as he continued in his letter, had so accustomed him to unhappiness and vileness and made him so indifferent to all the things of this world that he now felt he had almost nothing left to feel for what had once so deeply moved him. He had suffered so greatly during the war that his emotional stamina was completely exhausted and had built for itself a husk of deadness and apathy making him unfit for anything further. [141]

# IX

*One Must Renew Oneself Spiritually*
Of Illness and Misfortune
(1763-1786)

It was only his closest confidants to whom the King let on about his emotional helplessness. These rare moments were evoked, as often as not, by his little canine companions, as, for example, by the serious disorder of his she-dog Alkmene. In light of her suffering, even the death of August III, King of Poland and Elector of Saxony, was at first a relatively milder blow; this an historically explosive event, which, through the now open question of succession in Poland, would once again jeopardize the recently restored balance of power in Europe. Frederick wrote to his brother Henry in October 1763: *Now the King of Poland has died, like the fool he is! I'll confess to you I have no love for people who are always doing things at the wrong time. But I hope the new election will pass without unleashing new difficulties. I'm having trouble at home. My poor dog is just about to die. I must console myself with the thought that, if death does not spare the crowned heads, poor Alkmene should not expect a better fate.*[142]

The year 1763, now nearing its end, was ultimately the King's greatest year of triumph. He had stood his ground against superior enemy forces. His renown had grown enormously thanks to his military achievements, but also to the fact that Prussian coffers were less empty after the peace agreement than those of the other great powers. He even had the means for an initial redevelopment effort. Without concern for his own emotional liabilities, the King made a great personal effort to bring about an extraordinarily rapid restoration and renewal of his country – convinced that only a reinvigorated state had a chance of survival in the struggle among the European powers. His first move was to grant relief to those provinces that had suffered most in the war. In 1788 the royal Prussian Chief Consistorial Councilor Anton Friedrich Büsching noted in retrospect: *In 1763 he waived taxes for the province of Silesia for six months, a sum amounting to 978,200 thalers; he donated seventeen thousand horses to the province, which came to an estimated value of 340,000 thalers. ... The province of Pomerania had suffered much, but shortly after peace was restored, the King sent it the entire reserves of grain and flour left over in the wartime warehouses and a share of the provisions and freight horses that had returned from the war, which came to 12,327 animals. This royal gift had a value of 306,550 thalers; he also earmarked 1,363,000 thalers for the rebuilding of the houses, barns, cattle sheds that had burned down on the flatlands. The province of Neumark had lost roughly 2000 buildings, plus the majority of its horses, cows and sheep in the war; it also lacked even the bare minimum of grain to sustain people till the next harvest. The King redressed all these deficits. He had the burned-down buildings rebuilt, gave several villages between 6 and 700 thalers to use for purchasing draft oxen, had 68,866 sheep and*

*6442 horses, plus flour, grits, rye, barley, oats and peas distributed to the people. To the Kurmark communities that had been ravaged by the Russians he gave 300,000 thaler, ordering that the money be distributed only to subjects and peasants who had been harmed.*[143]

On September 19, 1763, the King signed a *confirmation of the purchase agreement concluded with the merchant Gotzkowsky concerning his bona fide porcelain factory in Berlin.*[144] Following the totally unexpected bankruptcy of Gotzkowsky, who had rendered outstanding service to Prussia in the development of top-quality porcelain, the King took over the management himself in order to save the beloved factory. Accordingly, the *Royal Prussian Porcelain Factory of Berlin* bore from then on a new trademark: The *G* in Gotzkowsky was replaced by the sceptre on the coat of arms of Electoral Brandenburg.

Meanwhile the King had also mandated construction of a large palace in Sanssouci Park. Placed a suitable distance from his vineyard house, relatives and highborn guests were to be housed here, and performances and conferences held. For himself he chose the little wing at the southern end of the *palais* for his private domain, far removed from official palace traffic. He used these strikingly small rooms, for example, whenever his siblings visited. Overall, the palace grounds, on such massive scale, were totally arresting and made a great impression on contemporaries. Many even believed that the King had the magnificent palace built only in order to demonstrate the economic strength of his country in the wake of the Seven Years' War.[145] In view of the scope of the New Palais, which with its forms expressive of courtly grandeur differed fundamentally from the modest Sanssouci Palace, the new authoritative European profile of Frederick the Great seemed to be manifesting itself. The fact is that construction had been planned for as early as the 1750's, but the Seven Years' War and the concentration of financial resources necessitated by it delayed the project's realization for years.

In close proximity to the Palace two other small buildings went up according to the King's specifications: the Temple of Antiquities for parts of his valuable antiquities collection and the Temple of Friendship in memory of his departed sister, with a larger-than-life statue of the Margravine and her favorite little dog *Folichon*. The execution of the statue was assigned to Johann Lorenz Wilhelm Räntz, a Bayreuth sculptor who had settled in Potsdam. Of course, Wilhelmine would no longer be represented in the garment of the Order, as in the template painting *Wilhelmine in Pilgertracht* (this out of reverence for the Freemasons' *Mopsorden* [Order of the Pug]), for Frederick's own relationship to the Freemasons had, over time, changed substantially. It had now been twenty years since he ceased being active in the lodge, rejecting the emerging secret-society and esoteric rituals of many lodges as silly little *follies*. Yet he retained an internal sympathy for the enlightened and humanitarian ideals of the communities and pledged himself to their protection in

Johann Lorenz Wilhelm Räntz, the renowned Bayreuth sculptor, who himself had worked for the Margravine, was commissioned by the King to create the marble statue *Wilhelmine as Roman philosopher* (1772-73)

Prussia for as long as he lived. Wilhelmine was to be immortalized in the Friendship Temple in the sense of the King's *Epistle* as *sister, whom to goddess I did raise.* She became a gentle Roman goddess, perhaps also a philosopher, who while reading a book pauses to reflect as she gazes pensively in the viewer's direction. In contrast to her rather virtuous presence in Anton Pesne's painting, here she is wearing an ancient, almost sensual garment that hugs her body, without a trace of ornamentation. What is more, the hem of her garment is rolled up above her Roman boot. This characteristic reverence of hers for the past underlay the sister's predilection for Roman history and philosophy. *Whether it be weakness or exaggerated veneration,* wrote Frederick to Voltaire, *I have done for my sister what Cicero had in mind for his Tullia, and had a Temple of Friendship erected in her honor … I often go there to think about all the losses and about the great happiness I once enjoyed.* [146]

After the end of the Seven Years' War, the fifty-one-year-old King was already feeling very much like an old man scarred by illness and misfortune. As with other vicissitudes of life, he also knew how to deal with his own malaises. He wrote to his former reader: *Life, my dear Darget, is a churlish affair when one gets old. One must decide either to die on the spot or watch oneself dwindle away bit by bit. Yet in all things there is a way to be happy; one must renew oneself spiritually, ignoring one's body and maintaining an inner cheerfulness right to the end of the play and strewing the final steps of the path with flowers.*[147]

The way the King chose to *renew himself spiritually* was necessarily different now than before 1756. Because of the deaths of important intimates, the old Sanssouci roundtable could no longer be reestablished. To be sure, he enjoyed now as he did then being together with colorful personalities, but in a different way than before the war when he could still be amused by others' caprice and vanity; now, after years of the most brutal experience of war, any sort of conceitedness became unbearable to him. Even the Marquis d'Argens was put off by this change in the King's disposition, the latter having nothing but stinging mockery now for his delicate sensibilities; the former, against Frederick's wishes, finally retiring to the provinces in bitterness, there to spend the evening of his life. There were now only a few individuals who could meet the King's high expectations; numbered among them were the quick-witted Baron Friedrich Melchior Grimm and the bookseller Nicolai, whom the King regarded as having an extraordinarily sharp mind and who, more importantly, said what others dared not utter. The King also valued very highly his daily walks with Lord Marshal Keith, whom upon his return from Scotland he even gifted with a house near Sanssouci, in order to keep him in his immediate vicinity. In gratitude, the recipient had the inscription, *Fridericus II. nobis haec otia fecit* affixed above the house's main entrance, a reference to a pastoral poem by Virgil. In the first *Eclogue*, the long-suffering shepherd Tityrus declares in a dialogue with the flute-playing shepherd Meliboeus, who has been driven from his land, that *deus nobis haec otia fecit*: God has created this peace for us – alluding to the idyllic spot in free nature on which both now live.

Living somewhat less idyllically, on Kochstraße 61-62 in Berlin and on his Wustrau estate, was another dear friend, General Hans Joachim von Zieten, who stood by the King's side during those last trying years of the Seven Years' War, not only militarily but also as a paternal friend. Also belonging to the innermost circle was his longtime companion from the crown-prince period, Baron Heinrich August de la Motte Fouqué, to whom Frederick had given the cathedral priory in Brandenburg in order to secure an income for the deserving officer, who had been seriously wounded in the Seven Years' War. The only trips the aging baron now undertook were to the King in Sanssouci, who was now leading a secluded life himself. Count Lehndorff wrote in his diary, *February 1764. The King has shut himself away in Sanssouci, all alone, to write his memoires.* [148] On October 12 of the same year, Nicolai noted: *The King now has a great love of painting and spends at least four (!) hours a day in his new gallery.* [149] This was a time he wished to spend completely undisturbed, excepting only the company of his favorite dog. His servants used his love of animals to bring pressing matters to his attention. They would stir up the other dogs waiting outside the gallery, inciting them to whine and scratch at the door for as long as it took to interrupt their master in his solitary viewing.

At this point, exuberant festivities and representational duties could no longer rouse the King's enthusiasm. Moreover, his health was compromised to the extent that he would go out of his way to avoid unnecessary exertions that did not serve the immediate welfare of the state. Of course, he continued to drill his regiment three times per week as always; on the other hand, when it came to the wedding of the heir to the throne, Frederick William, whom he regarded in any case as family *trash* for his dissolute lifestyle, his compromised health was reason enough to cancel his attendance. He limited his participation in wedding celebrations to a minimum and told his nephew, *As for the rest, my infirmities prevent me from taking part in any and all banquets.*[150] He seemed hardly capable of conforming any longer to a vapid courtly etiquette. Frederick wrote to the venerable Baron Heinrich August de la Motte Fouqué on April 25, 1765, *My dear friend! For five weeks I have had gout and hemorrhoids, worse than ever, and since the suffering is over and I am now beginning to recuperate, I have nothing more pressing to do than to send you this report on myself. ... You'll not be cross if I visit you on the way to Magdeburg.* On June 6 he added, *I will be at your place on the ninth at noon, my dear friend! I'll be quite alone, no formal meal or expenses required. Potluck, (pot-au-feu) taken literally, will suffice.*[151] Fouqué was one of his last remaining friends of youth. As expressions of sympathy, the King would regularly send the old baron little personal gifts, intended to make his life more comfortable: choice fruits from Sanssouci, truffles from France, hundred-year-old Hungarian wine, or, from *old-timer to old-timer,* a comfortable armchair with adjustable backrest. When the baron found walking difficult, he had a kind of wheelchair made specifically for him; as his hearing faded, he sent him special pipes to amplify sound; and even as his friend's ability to speak became a problem, Frederick invented a machine by means of which letters could be combined to supplement his words. The King cherished the few dear ones remaining to him, among these also his sisters, who corresponded regularly with him and frequently sought advice, even regarding problems with their spouses.

Upon the death of his sister Sophie, younger than he by seven years, who passed away as Margravine of Schwedt after an unhappy marriage and a long illness, he wrote to Countess Camas: *Our family seems to me to be a forest in which a hurricane has toppled the most beautiful trees and where one sees from time to time a branchless fir, barely surviving by holding fast to its roots, in order to witness the downfall of its environment and the devastation and destruction caused by the storm.*[152]

The Queen Mother and three siblings, August William, Wilhelmine and Sophie, had all died in the last twelve years. During those years Frederick had developed an especially intense relationship to his youngest, unmarried sister Amalie, a strong, willful personality who was a serious musician and composer. She was his equal in intelligence, in the refusal to compromise

The old General Fouqué in his wheelchair, commissioned for him by the King, during a visit to Sanssouci. Illustration by Adolph Menzel for Franz Kuglers *Geschichte Friedrichs des Großen*, 1868

and in sarcastic bite, and was the only relative he visited in her palace in Berlin with any regularity. Yet she received no preferential treatment in the will he drafted on Januuary 8, 1769, just prior to his 57th birthday, this to account for changed family circumstances. In thirty-three points the King mainly revised family affairs. Point number one, essentially unchanged, pertained to his own person and the procedure to be carried out following his demise. Once again he decreed: *I am to be buried at Sanssouci on top of the terraces, in a crypt I have had built for myself.*[153]

Between 1752 and 1769, the King stipulated no fewer than four times that he wished to be interred in the crypt. What he chose for himself he bestowed as well not only upon *Biche* but all his dogs; the terrain immediately surrounding the planted area and the crypt became their burial ground. By 1775 the historian of Potsdam's buildings, Matthias Oesterreich, had already registered six canine names.[154] By the time of the King's death in 1786, at least eleven dogs were buried there. In the first row: *Alkmene, Thisbe, Diana, Phillis, Thisbe, Bige. In the second row: Diana, Pax, Superbe, Hasenfuß and Amouretto.*

Each Italian greyhound received a sandstone plate with its name. The headstone for *Alkmene*, laid by the master stonemason Ludwig Trippel in August of 1775, cost the King 11 thalers and 12 cents from his private coffers. Frederick's reaction to the death of his beloved *Alkmene* was conveyed by his chamber hussar Schöning: *When He was notified of her death in Silesia, He ordered that her dead body be placed in His library room at Sanssouci, in the coffin in which she had been laid. Shortly after His return, He repaired there and gave free rein to His tears and sadness. The fact is, He had to tear himself away from the decomposing body, but He had it placed in the crypt on the grounds of Sanssouci House, the same brickwork crypt that He had had built for His own future corpse.*[155]

Frederick's personal physician Zimmermann described the incident somewhat differently. In his version the dog had already been buried by the time the King arrived and had to be exhumed as per his wish so that Frederick could take proper leave of him.[156]

In his biographical tale, *Tage des Königs* (Days of the King), of 1920, Bruno Frank describes this last encounter most movingly. Frank, who emigrated from Germany thirteen years after the novella's appearance, lauds therein precisely the oft-denigrated love of the King for his gracious dogs: *These dogs and his taste were as un-German as possible. They embodied everything his Prussia, his Mark, did not have, this coarse and cloudy land to which he remained banished. They called the breed Italian whippets, but they did not mean to him simply gaiety and the diaphanous sky of Florence; rather they were, as metaphor and as greeting, his free, artistically splendid Athens, his elegant, sylphlike Paris.*[157]

They were nearly all that was left to the King in his surroundings of tender propinquity, dainty sensuousness and playfulness. He now preferred to live with them and his little entourage in Sanssouci, his cloister.

In 1773 his flute instructor, Johann Joachim Quantz, died, who had also been his treasured musical companion for over three decades. Missing front teeth were now reason enough for the King to put away his flute for good. Even house concerts, which he could now participate in only as a listener, no longer gave him pleasure. The concert hall, once so lovingly appointed, was now no longer used in accord with its musical function. In 1774 Baron de la Motte Fouqué died, followed in 1778 by Lord Marshal Keith. It became lonely around Frederick; the intimate visits and daily walks fell away. Rooms reserved for his friends remained empty. The few rooms the King still used were in run-down condition, curtains, sofas and armchairs soiled and torn by the dogs. He attached no great importance to renovating the palace. He had other priorities. *I work a lot to distract myself and find that work brings me the most relief,* he had written to his sister as early as 1752. The building-up of his country and the continuing divisions among the European powers left him no other choice in any case. And yet, scholarship and art remained his most important *medicine.* He was, furthermore, the *roi philosophe*, who in the midst of turbulent events and before important decisions always reflected on the people, their fortunes and the influence of destiny and who with the help of philosophy also gave thought to the character of his state, in particular, how virtuous behavior might be encouraged and made to serve the welfare of the community. Once again he took up the treatise, *De Officis*, by Cicero, and occupied himself with the moral-humanitarian ideas of Voltaire, whom he had esteemed since earliest youth, and wrote essays himself on the nature of virtue. *As roi philosophe* he also recorded his political insights, which would be preserved for the heir apparent and posterity. In so doing, he imposed upon himself the obligation to regard events with the impartial view of the philosopher – and, in contrast to the memoir, distance himself from his own interior life, from his sufferings.

Focussed only on what was essential, the King led a life far beyond all courtly gallantry and decorative adornments. Not only had the gilt edges of the palace lost their luster over time and the silk upholstery become shabby in places, even in his immediate personal surroundings there was no longer a glittering court. Braided servants were a thing of the past. All that remained were a few chamber husars who oversaw household affairs. According to statements of contemporaries, the King's household resembled that of an old bachelor. The rooms showed a lack of order and cleanliness. Even his outward appearance was downright eccentric. After the Seven Years' War, he refused to wear gold, silver or jewelry on his clothing. He wore a uniform that was less than pressed, which, however, did not compromise the esteem he enjoyed among the public one jot. General von der Marwitz described a singular childhood experience from the year 1782, as Frederick the Great passed by him in a coach:

The King with two valets on the terrace of Sanssouci, by Daniel Nikolaus Chodowiecki

*I was at most one cubit away from the King, and it seemed to me as if I were looking at God Almighty. He looked straight ahead through the front window. He had on a very old three-cornered mounted hat whose upright rear brim he had turned forward and loosened its tie, so that the brim hung down in front, protecting him from the sun.*

*The hat cordons had come loose and were dancing around the let-down brim; the white general's feather on his hat was tattered and dirty; the simple blue mounting, along with red lapels, collar and gold shoulder knot, old and dusty, the yellow vest full of tobacco; — he also had on black velvet pants.*[158]

With all his neglect of externals, the King, as always, placed the greatest value on an orderly daily routine. In summer he had himself awakened around four a.m. and in winter around five. In the morning, petitions received were to be processed on the same day. During meal times he enjoyed stimulating conversation in his small circle on the most varied subjects: on Bacon and Newton; on the composer Willibald Gluck, whose work he did not care for; on Racine, whose *Mithridate* he had recited after the defeat at Hochkirch; on Goethe's *Werther*, which baffled him; or, on the other hand, on Lessing, whose plays he found noteworthy. He devoted the afternoons to his own writing or his correspondence; he spent one to two evening hours with his reader. After dismissing the latter, he would retire to his bedchamber with its simple field cot. Here he was surrounded by the things he loved most, by his favorite dog, which was permitted to share the bed with him, and by his favorite books, which always stood at his disposal on tables next to the bed within reach. It was only from his bedroom that access to his circular library was possible, this through a secret mirrored door, the threshold of which no one was permitted to cross without his express approval. With a collection of 2,288 volumes, it was the most comprehensive of his seven palace libraries and was considered the most beautiful royal private library of the 18<sup>th</sup> century. The King had all volumes acquired for Sanssouci bound in the reddish-brown-hued leather of native domestic goats and marked on their spines with a golden V, the sign for *vigne* (vineyard). The office of librarian was regarded as a position of unparalleled trust. This position was held until the beginning of 1780 by Baron Henri de Catt, who had also been Frederick's reader since March of 1758. Alas, after twenty-one years of activity at court there occurred an irrevocable breach of trust, as the later reader, Marchese Lucchesini, reported: *One night sleep eludes the old King. He wants to be read to a while longer and so goes looking for Catt in his room. He finds the latter not alone, but in the arms of a dancing girl, whom Catt has helped to slip in from the garden. The King goes back in silence. The next day the reader is dismissed: "If I grant Her Majesty and not a single lady of my court permission to enter the vigne, then He [i.e., My Lord] must understand that my command is likewise applicable to his whore!*[159]

Baron de Catt was replaced by the Abbé Duval du Peyrau, whom, however, the King could bear for only a few weeks. In a letter of March 26, 1780, he expressed his pique to d'Alembert: *This man gives me lectures on theological absurdities, and I'm supposed to profit and learn something from them! I chased the canaille off to hell. What am I to do now?*[160] D'Alembert recommended another reader, the twenty-nine-year-old Italian Count Lucchesini, and advised the King to persuade himself of the young man's quality as soon as possible. Joachim von Kürenberg describes their first meeting based on Lucchesini's diary entries: *It is the 3rd of May, 1780. Meanwhile the King has invited the Marchese to Potsdam for the Spring review. For hours already the nearly seventy-year-old man sits bent over on his favorite horse, "Condé," without Lucchesini's having had an opportunity to greet the King. ... Finally the King dismounts. Pacing back and forth, he gives an officer a few instructions. During the exchange, "Condé" trots along just behind the King, snuffling his coat pockets, from which the horse pulls out bits of melon and fig. The King is not distracted by this; he only calls out a few words now and then to his dog, such as: "á gauche, Alcmène!" ... The King calls to Lucchesini: "Where has the Count been dallying for so long?" "I've travelled through Germany, Majesty!" – The Marchese wants to explain further, but the little creature has run up to him, is now wagging its tail cheerfully and jumps up on him. The King, quite amazed by the otherwise "so prudish Alcmène," stares at the Marchese as though at a rare bird, and finally smiles: "Qu'est-ce que ça, Alcmène? Does she want to play the interesseuse? – Eh bien, Marquis! If Alcmène says yes, who am I to contradict! I hope the Marquis will not stand in any less favor with me!"* [161]

On this version, Lucchesini had *Alcmène* to thank for getting the King to accept him so easily. In his first letter from Sanssouci, the Marquis wrote to his former teacher Spallanzani:

*Potsdam, May 12, 1780.*
*Dear Maestro!*
*As you no doubt will already have heard from the courier of the Sardinian envoy, I have been selected by the King to be his reader. ... My duties are most pleasant and consist in dining with the King every day and extending the literary conversations, begun inter scyphos, often by two to three hours. The King assures me over and over of his full confidence. I hope to meet the mathematician La Grange soon, as in general there are still plenty of scholars living here and in Berlin who would do honor to any Italian university. Of course, many luminaries have either died or moved away, so that it has become very lonely around the old King.* [162]

To be sure, Lucchesini also noted that this loneliness referred solely to people; his dogs were for Frederick, as always, loyal companions. The fewer the intimates there were in whom he could confide and the more he believed he could see through the shallowness and hypocrisy of human beings, the more tenderly he turned to these guileless, sensitive creatures. They never tired or bothered him – on the contrary, he frequently gave them his undivided attention, even on important occasions. The Marquis himself became convinced of this in the year 1783. As he tells it in his diary, Lucchesini, in the King's company, was scheduled to attend an attention-getting experiment of the physicist Archard of the Berlin Academy, who was planning to sail up into the sky in a balloon. Frederick had it in mind to follow the exciting event from his terrace in Sanssouci. When Lucchesini arrived at the palace at the appointed time, to his amazement there was no one on the terrace. In the adjutant's room he found only the agitated footman Neumann: *Last night Thisbe suddenly passed away. The King's spirit is extremely low and he does not wish to be disturbed. His Majesty wept, something that did not occur even upon the death of the Queen of Sweden [his sister Ulrike].*[163] The Marchese thereafter left the palace, but was summoned to the King again that afternoon, and found the latter waiting for him impatiently. Lucchesini was to accompany him on a coach ride through the park. First, without exchanging a word, they rode to the pheasant close. The King then turned to his companion: *Autumn is coming, Marquis! The earth reeks of decay; soon we'll have to leave the vigne! … It must surprise you that an old man like me could lose his heart to a little dog. For fourteen years Thisbe was my constant companion; she was loyal to me, like that Queen of Babylon whose name I gave her. Perhaps she was bewitched! There was many a time I believed it! When I couldn't sleep at night, she lay next to me and looked at me so strangely – like a good person! Those eyes, Marquis, I'll never be able to forget them!* [164]

South of the New Palace Carl von Gotard had erected the Friendship Temple. As a model, he took the Apollo Temple of Wenzeslaus von Knobelsdorff, which had been built in 1735 in Neuruppin by order of the Crown Prince. As early as then, young Frederick had honored his sister as *Protectress of the Arts*.

As they conversed, the King and the Marchese reached the Friendship Temple. *Today is a somber day, Herr von Lucchesini! A great solennité funèbre. Unfortunately you didn't know the Margravine. I had this temple built here in her memory! Everything decays, the greenery, animals and – people! – And the question arises, to what end, what is the point of it all! After inner struggles we pour out our feelings to the creatures of nature at large, only in order to receive them back one day in pain.* [165]

Soon thereafter they returned to Sanssouci. Lucchesini also described the end of this excursion: *The sedan chair is waiting at the foot of the outside staircase. The King has himself carried up the steps unaccompanied. He gets out on the highest terrace and proceeds to the freshly formed mound over Thisbe. – At a height of 200 meters, Herr Archard's balloon now floats over Potsdam. People in the city are ecstatic. Up here Herr Archard is forgotten – for Thisbe – Thisbe is dead!*[166]

Clearly his dogs were far more important to him than all the balloon flights in the world. Even at the most lavish dinners in the Berlin palace, Frederick's concern was primarily for his Italian greyhounds. The Marchese Lucchesini was witness to this at an official supper in December of 1784 and recorded the following in his diary: *While at table he often uses his fingers instead of a fork. … With his fingers he moves the meat for his favorite dog from his plate onto the tablecloth, to let it cool. This tends to soil both tablecloth and napkin heavily; and since, moreover, his wine and water overflow every now and then and he badly spills his snuff tobacco, when dinner is over one can always recognize the place where he ate. It is always eight courses that are served, four French, two Italian and two special dishes. The menu card must lie at the head of the King's place. … After supper the King takes a crayon and makes crosses after those dishes he enjoyed. Sometimes he asks those present for their opinion. … After that the King often asks to see the dogs' menu, to monitor it. Guests who have used the occasion to visit the Italian greyhounds are astonished by the servants, who have been ordered to address the animals in French with the formal "you": "[formal:] Come on, Superbe, [formal:] eat something. [formal:] You haven't eaten enough yet!", or "Pax, [formal:] take it easy. [formal:] You'll get sick, if you keep gobbling your food!"* [167]

Even Paulig, Frederick's biographer, was somewhat taken aback in reporting on the respect the aging King insisted be accorded the dogs: *"If the dogs were taken for a ride, they would always have the best seats, on velvet pillows. The servant minding them sat on the rear seat and had to address the beasts with 'Sie' [i.e., formally]."* [168]

The capricious Italian greyhounds, especially the presiding favorite, were on the whole the only sentient beings capable of focusing the King's complete attention on themselves, like little absolutistic rulers. He could refuse them nothing; he granted them what he never would have arrogated to himself. As an enlightened monarch, he gave the monarchy a new foundation, which distinguished him from all the absolutist rulers of his time. To the end of his life, he would see himself as the first servant of his state, as *premier domestique*, and would subordinate himself to this mission with almost unbelievable energy and self-discipline, despite all misfortune and sorrow.

# X
*Where is Superbe?*
The Death of the King
(1786)

Frederick was now seventy-four years old. He would have only a few more months to live. The cabinet secretaries, who would normally assemble before the King in the morning between six and seven o'clock, were now summoned two hours earlier, between four and five o'clock. *My condition,* as he said, announcing this inconvenient change in schedule, *compels me to inflict this annoyance on you, which will not last long. My life is on the wane; I must use the time I have left well. It belongs not to me, but to the state.*[169]

His Cabinet Minister Ewald Friedrich von Hertzberg reported the following to the French envoy von der Goltz:

*Berlin, 11 April 1786. The King's health is more and more on the decline; every day one expects the worst, although he takes care of business as always.*

*Berlin, 25 April 1786. The King has been at Sanssouci for six days. He's gone for daily jaunts of a few miles in the coach and has also twice gone out riding. He even gears up for the reviews, but in the opinion of the doctors, his life continues to hover in the gravest danger.*

*Berlin, 30 May 1786. The King continues to bear up wonderfully.*

*He's working more than ever, though his condition remains quite critical. While he was working yesterday*

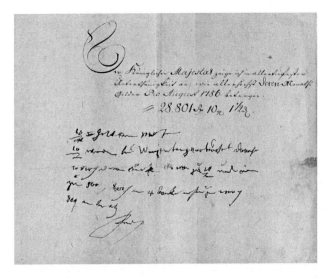

Three days before his death, on August 14, 1786, the King issued this final decree by his own hand.

*morning at 4 o'clock with his Cabinet Secretary Stelter, the latter had a stroke, which led to his death shortly thereafter. The King had his body removed and another secretary brought in, with whom he continued working.*

Twelve days before Frederick's death, Minister Herzberg wrote to the Princess of Orange, sister of the heir apparent Frederick William: *The King's condition changes from day to day. He has dropsy from his feet going up into his body. He treats himself and believes he'll live a few more years. The doctors he occasionally consults give him a few months at most, assuming a stroke doesn't snatch him away. He doesn't move from his chair, since he can't lie in bed. He takes care of all affairs with his usual energy and a covetousness excluding all others.* [170]

The King was well aware of his situation. In a final private letter to his sister Philippine Charlotte, the widowed Duchess of Braunschweig, he summarized on August 10, a week before his death: *The Hanoverian doctor was just giving himself airs, my good sister; the truth is, however, that he did me no good at all. The old must give way to the young, so that each generation has freedom of movement; and life, if we follow its course closely, consists in our seeing our fellows die and be born!* [171]

His own relatives, his consort Elisabeth Christine, whom he had seen for the last time eight months earlier, his siblings and even the Crown Prince – to these Frederick would grant no further opportunity to see him. The circle of those whose company he could tolerate became smaller and smaller. He mistrusted his entourage, whom like Minister Hertzberg he regarded – not without reason – as being on the side of his nephew, the future King, whom he held in low esteem. His love was reserved for his dogs exclusively. They alone were allowed to be really close to him and to remain with him till the end.

Even three days before his death, on Monday, August 14, he made an effort to carry out his duties as King. On the following morning, however, contrary to custom, he did not awaken until 11 o'clock, as his doctor, Selle, recorded in a medical report; still, he gave

The King died in an armchair, which he had had made for himself weeks earlier. Because of his pains, he could no longer lie down. (painting by Christian Bernhard Rode, 1786)

the requisite orders to the waiting generals and secretaries. Finally, on Wednesday morning, those showing up at the appointed hour were given the directive, *the secretaries are to wait*. The King's powers had further deteriorated; he found himself in a kind of twilight state with no more than brief periods of alertness. Present in his chamber were, by turns, the chamber hussars Schöning and Neumann, the chamber menial Strützki and *Superbe*, who lay on a footstool right next to the King. On Schöning's account, it was the little dog that was the object of the dying man's final alert moment. In the early morning of August 17, around 1 o'clock, the King missed his dog: *… where is Superbe; let her get back on her chair.* [172]

When the by now extremely weakened monarch noticed that the animal was shivering with cold – as was he himself – he gave the order, now scarcely audible, to cover *Superbe* with pillows. That is said to have been his last conscious utterance.

A little later, following a severe fit of coughing, he only mumbled, *La montagne est passée, nous irons mieux* – we are over the mountain; it will go better for us. [173]

At 2:20 a.m. Frederick II, called *the Great*, died.

# XI
## Epilogue

Immanuel Kant praised the King as *[he] who ...left everyone free to make use of his own reason in all matters having to do with conscience,* and described the Age of Enlightenment as Frederick's century. [174]

Johann Wolfgang von Goethe honored him posthumously in an *Elegy*:

> *He who stands firm when all others waver –*
> *He commands his people and governs the masses of men.*
> *Such a one did you recently witness,*
> *Being borne up to the gods from whom he descended.*
> *Looking up to him*
> *All the world's people, with saddened gaze.* [175]

The new King of Prussia being an exception, he having carried on a long-standing – and not very complimentary – correspondence with Minister Hertzberg concerning his old, obstinate uncle. Frederick had issued many testamentary decrees making it clear that he wanted to be laid to rest in the crypt at Sanssouci. The heir to the throne denied him this wish. Frederick William II did not have the deceased King interred among his beloved Italian greyhounds in the little, by now moldered, burial chamber, but rather in the Garrison Church Potsdam, beside his despotic father, the *Soldier King* – this for reasons of prestige.

As though the crypt were intending to call to mind the legacy of the decedent, its entrance collapsed between 1830 and 1840. The same thing happened again on January 24, 1860, the 148th birthday of Frederick II.[176]

It was not until 205 years after his death-day that Prince Louis Ferdinand of Prussia fulfilled the testamentary decree of Frederick the Great.

On August 17, 1991, the King found his final resting place in the crypt at Sanssouci – right next to *Biche, Alkmene, Thisbe, Superbe, Pax* and his other beloved dogs.

*Quand je serai là, je serai sans souci –*
When I am there, I will be without care.

# Endnotes

1  Joachim v. Kürenberg, Der letzte Vertraute Friedrichs des Großen – Marchese Lucchesini, Berlin 1933, 62.
2  Reinhold Koser, quoted in Paul Seidel, Friedrich der Große und die bildende Kunst, Berlin and Leipzig 1922, 18.
3  Ingeborg Weber-Kellermann, ed., Wilhelmine von Bayreuth, Frankfurt a.M. 1990, 31.
4  Weber-Kellermann, loc. cit., 45.
5  Quoted in Franz Kugler, Geschichte Friedrichs des Großen, Leipzig 1856, 17.
6  Helmut Börsch-Supan, Die Gemälde Antoine Pesnes in den Berliner Schlössern, Berlin 1982, 28.
7  Friedrich Rudolf Paulig, Friedrich der Große. König von Preußen, Frankfurt a. d. O. 1910, 11.
8  Walter Stengel, Freundschaft mit Hunden, Berlin 1960, 23.
9  Stengel, loc. cit., 23ff.
10  Weber-Kellermann, loc. cit., 96.
11  D. Anton Friederich Büsching, Character Friedrichs des zweyten, Königs von Preussen, 2nd ed., Halle 1788, 179.
12  Paulig, loc. cit., 18.
13  Quoted in Christian Graf von Krockow and Karl-Heinz Jürgens, Friedrich der Große, Lebensbilder, Bergisch Gladbach 1986, 28.
14  Kugler, loc. cit., 28.
15  Weber-Kellermann, loc. cit., 96.
16  Büsching, loc. cit., 179.
17  Paulig, loc. cit., 23.
18  Weber-Kellermann, loc. cit., 142.
19  Ibid., 146.
20  Ibid., 147f.
21  Paulig, loc. cit., 36.
22  Weber-Kellermann, loc. cit., 233.
23  Quoted in Günther Wolff, Friedrich der Große. Krankheiten und Tod, Mannheim 2000, 39.
24  Weber-Kellermann, loc. cit., 283.
25  Kirsten Heckmann-Janz, Sibylle Kretschmer and Friedrich Wilhelm Prinz von Preußen, eds., "… solange wir zu zweit sind." Friedrich der Große und Wilhelmine Markgräfin von Bayreuth in Briefen, Munich 2003, 36.
26  Heckmann-Janz, Kretschmer and Prinz von Preußen, loc. cit., 55.
27  Ibid., 100.
28  Gustav Berthold Volz, ed., Friedrich der Große und Wilhelmine von Baireuth, vol. I, Leipzig 1924, 321.

29 Quoted in Hans-Joachim Giersberg, Schloß Sanssouci, Berlin 2005, 19.
30 Quoted in Wolfgang Röd, ed., Die deutsche Philosophie im Zeitalter der Aufklärung, in Geschichte der Philosophie VIII. Die Philosophie der Neuzeit 2, Munich 1984, 251.
31 Quoted in Gustav Berthold Volz, ed., Friedrich der Große im Spiegel seiner Zeit, vol. I, Berlin 1926-27, 81.
32 Quoted in Giersberg, Schloß Sanssouci, loc. cit., 15.
33 Quoted in Titus Malms, Das Freimaurertum Friedrichs des Großen zwischen Ideal und kritischer Distanz, in Dieter Alfter, ed., Friedrich der Große. König zwischen Pflicht und Neigung, Bad Pyrmont 2004, 56.
34 Quoted in Volz, Friedrich der Große im Spiegel seiner Zeit, loc. cit., 67.
35 Quoted in Giersberg, Schloß Sanssouci, loc. cit., 15.
36 Quoted in Volz, Friedrich der Große im Spiegel seiner Zeit, loc. cit., 119.
37 Stengel, loc. cit., 23.
38 Friedrich Benninghoven, Helmut Börsch-Supan and Iselin Gundermann, Friedrich der Große, Berlin 1986, 64.
39 See Johannes Kunisch, Friedrich der Große. Der König und seine Zeit, Munich 2004, 174.
40 Gustav Berthold Volz, Briefwechsel Friedrichs des Großen mit seinem Bruder August Wilhelm, Leipzig n.d., 47f.
41 Heckmann-Janz, Kretschmer and Prinz von Preußen, loc. cit., 165.
42 Ibid., 179f.
43 Ibid., 180. Letter of May 15, 1744.
44 Ibid., 180.
45 StA Marburg, Best. 118a, Nr. 3326. Letter from Seip of June 5, 1744.
46 Hans Droysen, Der Briefwechsel Friedrichs des Großen mit der Gräfin Camas und dem Baron Fouqué, v. I, Veröffentlichungen aus den Archiven Preussischer Kulturbesitz, vol. I, Berlin 1967, 7.
47 Droysen, loc. cit., 10f.
48 Kugler, loc. cit., 192.
49 Volz, Briefwechsel, loc. cit., 1
50 Paulig, loc. cit., 125, quotes the name "Biche" as part of the letter text as well.
51 Johannes Richter, Die Briefe Friedrichs des Großen an seinen vormaligen Kammerdiener Fredersdorf, Berlin 1926, 53.
52 Richter, loc. cit., 53f.
53 Paulig, loc. cit., 125.
54 Richter, loc. cit., 75.
55 Ibid., 76.
56 Jürgen Ziechmann, Geschichtsklitterung um Friedrich II.: Der zweite Aufenthalt Friedrichs in Bad Pyrmont vom 17. Mai bis 8. Juni 1746 in der späteren lokalen Berichterstattung, 185, in Jürgen Fredmann, ed., Fridericianische Miniaturen I, Bremen 1988.

57 Volz, Briefwechsel, loc. cit., 83.
58 Heckmann-Janz, Kretzschmer and Prinz von Preußen, loc. cit., 213ff. See also Volz, Friedrich der Große und Wilhelmine von Bayreuth, loc. cit., 140ff.
59 Heckmann-Janz, Kretschmer and Prinz von Preußen, loc. cit., 215ff. See also Volz, Friedrich der Große und Wilhelmine von Bayreuth, loc. cit., 142ff.
60 Volz, Friedrich der Große und Wilhelmine von Baireuth, loc. cit., 144f.
61 Ibid., 145f.
62 Peter O. Krückmann, Paradies des Rokoko, vol. I. of Das Bayreuth der Markgräfin Wilhelmine, Munich and New York 1998, 50f.
63 Paulig, loc. cit., 345f.
64 Volz, Briefwechsel, loc. cit., 99.
65 See Georg Poensgen, Antoine Pesne, Berlin 1958, 67f.
66 Volz, Briefwechsel, loc. cit., 107.
67 Volz, Friedrich der Große im Spiegel seiner Zeit, vol. I, loc. cit., 213.
68 Baetke, loc. cit., 192.
69 Volz, Briefwechsel, loc. cit., 129f.
70 Ibid., 130.
71 Ibid., 144, facsimile of the letter of guardianship.
72 Ibid., 143.
73 Ibid., 143f.
74 Baetke, loc. cit., 193.
75 Ibid., 194.
76 Volz, Briefwechsel, loc. cit., 181.
77 Volz, Friedrich der Große und Wilhelmine von Baireuth, loc. cit., 213f.
78 Ibid., 215ff.
79 Charlotte Pangels, Friedrich der Große. Bruder, Freund und König, Munich 1998, 207.
80 Hans-Joachim Giersberg, Die Ruhestätte Friedrichs des Großen zu Sanssouci, 2nd ed., Berlin 1992, 39.
81 Volz, Friedrich der Große und Wilhelmine von Baireuth, loc. cit., 217f.
82 Ibid., 237f.
83 Ibid., 239.
84 Ibid., 241.
85 Paulig, loc. cit., 126.
86 According to Nicolai, 1789, Anekdoten von Friedrich II., qtd. in Volz, Friedrich der Große im Spiegel seiner Zeit, vol. I, loc. cit., 215: "Wenn ich dort bin, werde ich ohne Sorge sein."
87 Karl Büchner, ed., Lukrez: De rerum natura. Welt aus Atomen, Stuttgart 1973, 238.

88  Büsching, loc. cit., 22f.

89  Hildegard von Bingen, Naturkunde. Das Buch von dem inneren Wesen der verschiedenen Naturen in der Schöpfung, Salzburg 1989, 131.

90  Heckmann-Janz, Kretschmer and Prinz von Preußen, loc. cit., 109.

91  Ibid., 121.

92  Paulig, loc. cit., 126.

93  Quoted in Paul Münch, "Die Differenz zwischen Mensch und Tier," in Paul Münch, ed., Tiere und Menschen, Paderborn 1998, 328.

94  Quoted in Münch, loc. cit., 332.

95  Quoted in Rainer Walz, "Die Verwandtschaft von Mensch und Tier," in Münch, loc. cit., 318.

96  Richter, loc. cit., 213.

97  Ibid., 240.

98  Paulig, loc. cit., 319.

99  Volz, Briefwechsel, loc. cit, 194.

100  Richter, loc. cit., 315f.

101  Ibid., 366f.

102  Heckmann-Janz, Kretschmer and Prinz von Preußen, loc. cit., 248. Also Volz, Friedrich der Große und Wilhelmine von Baireuth, loc. cit., 303f.

103  Weber-Kellermann, loc. cit., 461f.

104  Volz, Briefwechsel, loc. cit., 247: Potsdam, Feb. 12, 1756.

105  Haug von Kuenheim, Aus den Tagebüchern des Grafen Lehndorff, Berlin, 1982, 80f.

106  Thomas Carlyle, Friedrich der Große, Berlin n.d., 484.

107  Heckmann-Janz, Kretschmer and Prinz von Preußen, loc. cit., 268.

108  Volz, Friedrich der Große und Wilhelmine von Baireuth, loc. cit, 361.

109  Volz, Briefwechsel, loc. cit., 295.

110  Ibid., 297f.

111  Paul Seidel, Friedrich der Große und die bildende Kunst, Berlin and Leipzig 1922, 189.

112  Rainer Michaelis, Antoine Pesne, Berlin 2003, 12.

113  Kuenheim, loc. cit., 94.

114  Heckmann-Janz, Kretschmer and Prinz von Preußen, loc. cit., 279. Letter of September 17, 1757.

115  Kuenheim, loc. cit., 100.

116  Quoted in Giersberg, Die Ruhestätte Friedrichs des Großen zu Sanssouci, loc. cit., 44.

117  Hans Schumann, Mein lieber Marquis! Friedrich der Große, sein Briefwechsel mit Jean-Baptiste d'Argens während d. Siebenjährigen Krieges, Zürich 1985, 89f.

118  Richter, loc.cit., 24.

119 Kuenheim, loc. cit., 94f.
120 Quoted in Giersberg, Die Ruhestätte Friedrichs des Großen zu Sanssouci, loc. cit., 34f.
121 Jean-Paul Bled, Frédéric le Grand, Paris 2004, 398.
122 Volz, Briefwechsel, loc.cit., 300.
123 Quoted in Giersberg, Die Ruhestätte Friedrichs des Großen zu Sanssouci, loc. cit., 44.
124 Volz, Friedrich der Große und Wilhelmine von Baireuth, loc. cit., 448f.
125 Carlyle, loc. cit., 569.
126 Schumann, loc. cit., 106f.
127 Carlyle, loc. cit., 634.
128 Paulig, loc. cit., 265.
129 Carlyle, loc. cit., 680.
130 Ibid., 679.
131 Ibid., 683.
132 Paulig, loc. cit, 270.
133 Schumann, loc. cit., 346.
134 Max Hein, ed., Briefe Friedrichs des Großen, vol. II, Berlin 1914, 109.
135 Quoted in Winfried Baer, Ilse Baer and Suzanne Großkopf-Knaack, Von Gotzkowsky zur KPM, Berlin 1986, 68f.
136 Friedrich Benninghoven, Helmut Börsch-Supan and Iselin Gundermann, Friedrich der Große, Berlin 1986, 224.
137 Paulig, loc. cit., 274.
138 Droysen, loc. Cit., 44.
139 Quoted in Benninghoven, Börsch-Supan and Iselin Gundermann, loc. cit., 227.
140 Schumann, loc. cit., 375.
141 Ibid., 355.
142 Quoted in Christian Graf von Krockow, Die preußischen Brüder, 3rd ed., Stuttgart 1998, 160.
143 Büsching, loc. cit., 216f.
144 Quoted in Baer, Baer and Großkopf-Knaack, loc. cit., 76.
145 Seidel, loc. cit., 122.
146 Quoted in Gustav Berthold Volz, ed., Das Sans-Souci Friedrichs des Großen, Berlin and Leipzig 1926, 82.
147 Quoted in Benninghoven, Börsch-Suppan and Gundermann, loc. cit., 230.
148 Kuenheim, loc. cit., 151.
149 Quoted in Seidel, loc. cit., 166.
150 Quoted in Benninghoven, Börsch-Supan and Gundermann, loc. cit., 228.
151 Droysen, loc. cit., 65f.
152 Ibid., 51.

153 Giersberg, Die Ruhestätte Friedrichs des Großen zu Sanssouci, loc. cit., 44f.
154 See Giersberg, Die Ruhestätte Friedrichs des Großen zu Sanssouci, loc. cit., 36.
155 Büsching, loc. cit., 23.
156 See Stengel, loc. cit., 15.
157 Bruno Frank, "Tage des Königs," Berlin 1924, 142.
158 Carlyle, loc. cit., 724.
159 Joachim von Kürenberg, Der letzte Vertraute Friedrichs des Großen, Marchese Lucchesini, Berlin 1933, 34.
160 Kürenberg, loc. cit., 35.
161 Ibid., 35f.
162 Ibid., 37.
163 Ibid., 62.
164 Ibid., 62f.
165 Ibid., 63.
166 Ibid., 64.
167 Ibid., 78f.
168 Paulig, loc. cit., 126.
169 Quoted in Kugler, loc. cit., 505.
170 Gustav Berthold Volz, ed., Friedrich der Große im Spiegel seiner Zeit, vol. III, Berlin 1926-27, 227ff.
171 Carlyle, loc. cit., 738.
172 Kürenberg, loc. cit., 93.
173 See Carlyle, loc. cit., 74.
174 Theodor Schieder, Friedrich der Große, Berlin and Munich 2002, 490.
175 Volz, Friedrich der Große im Spiegel seiner Zeit, vol. 3, loc. cit., 277.
176 Giersberg, Die Ruhestätte Friedrichs des Großen zu Sanssouci, loc. cit., 19.

# References

**Baer**, Winfried, Ilse Baer and Suzanne Großkopf-Knaack, *Von Gotzkowsky zur KPM*, Berlin 1986.

**Benninghoven**, Friedrich, Helmut Börsch-Supan and Iselin Gundermann, *Friedrich der Große*, Berlin 1986.

**Bingen**, Hildegard von, *Naturkunde. Das Buch von dem inneren Wesen der verschiedenen Naturen in der Schöpfung*, Salzburg 1989.**Bled**, Jean-Paul, *Frédéric le Grand*, Paris 2004.

Börsch-Supan, Helmut, *Die Gemälde Anton Pesnes in den Berliner Schlößern*, Berlin 1982.

**Büchner**, Karl, ed., *Lukrez: De rerum natura. Welt aus Atomen*, Stuttgart 1973.

**Büsching**, D. Anton Friedrich, *Charakter Friedrichs des zweiten, Königs von Preußen*, 2nd ed., Halle 1788.

**Carlyle**, Thomas, *Friedrich der Große*, Berlin n.d.

**Droysen**, Hans, *Der Briefwechsel Friedrichs des Großen mit der Gräfin Camas und dem Baron Fouqué*, v. I, Veröffentlichungen aus den Archiven Preußischer Kulturbesitz, vol. I, Berlin 1967.

**Frank**, Bruno, *Tage des Königs*, Berlin 1924.

**Giersberg**, Hans-Joachim, *Die Ruhestätte Friedrichs des Großen zu Sanssouci*, 2nd ed., Berlin 1992. *Schloß Sanssouci*, Berlin 2005.

**Heckmann-Janz**, Kirsten, Sibylle Kretschmer and Friedrich Wilhelm Prinz von Preußen, eds., *"… solange wir zu zweit sind." Friedrich der Große und Wilhelmine Markgräfin von Bayreuth in Briefen*, Munich 2003.

**Hein**, Max, ed., *Briefe Friedrichs des Großen*, v. II, Berlin 1914

**Krockow**, Christian Graf von, *Die preußischen Brüder*, 3rd ed., Stuttgart 1998.

**Krockow**, Christian Graf von and Karl-Heinz Jürgens, *Friedrich der Große, Lebensbilder*, Bergisch Gladbach 1986.

**Krückmann**, Peter O., *Paradies des Rokoko*, v. I., Das Bayreuth der Markgräfin Wilhelmine, Munich and New York 1998.

**Kuenheim**, Haug von, *Aus den Tagebüchern des Grafen Lehndorff*, Berlin 1982.

**Kugler**, Franz, *Geschichte Friedrichs des Großen*, Leipzig 1856.

**Kunisch**, Johannes, *Friedrich der Große. Der König und seine Zeit*, Munich 2004.

**Kürenberg**, Joachim v., *Der letzte Vertraute Friedrichs des Großen – Marchese Lucchesini*, Berlin 1933.

**Malms**, Titus, "Das Freimaurertum Friedrichs des Großen zwischen Ideal und kritischer Distanz," in Dieter Alfter, ed., *Friedrich der Große. König zwischen Pflicht und Neigung*, Bad Pyrmont 2004.

**Michaelis**, Rainer, *Antoine Pesne*, Berlin 2003.

**Münch**, Paul, "Die Differenz zwischen Mensch und Tier," in Paul Münch, ed., *Tiere und Menschen*, Paderborn 1998.

**Pangels**, Charlotte, *Friedrich der Große. Bruder, Freund und König*, Munich 1998.

**Paulig**, Friedrich Rudolf, *Friedrich der Große. König von Preußen*, Frankfurt a. d. O. 1910.

**Poensgen**, Georg, *Antoine Pesne*, Berlin 1958.

**Richter**, Johannes, *Die Briefe Friedrichs des Großen an seinen vormaligen Kammerdiener Fredersdorf*, Berlin 1926.

**Röd**, Wolfgang, ed., *Die deutsche Philosophie im Zeitalter der Aufklärung*, in Geschichte der Philosophie VIII, Die Philosophie der Neuzeit 2, Munich 1984.

**Schieder**, Theodor, *Friedrich der Große*, Berlin and Munich 2002.

**Schumann**, Hans, *Mein lieber Marquis! Friedrich der Große, sein Briefwechsel mit Jean-Baptiste d'Argens während d. Siebenjährigen Krieges*, Zurich 1985.

**Seidel**, Paul, *Friedrich der Große und die bildende Kunst*, Berlin and Leipzig 1922.

**Stengel**, Walter, *Freundschaft mit Hunden*, Berlin 1960.

**Volz**, Gustav Berthold, ed., *Friedrich der Große und Wilhelmine von Baireuth*, v. I, Leipzig 1924.

**Volz**, Gustav Berthold, ed., *Das Sans-Souci Friedrichs des Großen*, Berlin and Leipzig 1926.

**Volz**, Gustav Berthold, ed., *Friedrich der Große im Spiegel seiner Zeit*, vols. I and III, Berlin 1926-27.

**Volz**, Gustav Berthold, *Briefwechsel Friedrichs des Großen mit seinem Bruder August Wilhelm*, Leipzig n.d.

**Weber-Kellermann**, Ingeborg, ed., *Wilhelmine von Bayreuth*, Frankfurt a.M. 1990.

**Wolff**, Günther, *Friedrich der Große. Krankheiten und Tod*, Mannheim 2000.

**Ziechmann**, Jürgen, "Geschichtsklitterung um Friedrich II.: Der zweite Aufenthalt Friedrichs in Bad Pyrmont vom 17. Mai bis 8. Juni 1746 in der späteren lokalen Berichterstattung," 185, in Jürgen Fredmann, ed., *Fridericianische Miniaturen* I, Bremen 1988.

# Aus dem Programm von PalmArtPress

*John Berger / Liane Birnberg*
**garden on my cheek**
ISBN: 978-3-941524-77-4
Kunst mit Lyrik, 90 Seiten, Klappenbroschur, Englisch

*Reid Mitchell*
**Sell Your Bones**
ISBN: 978-3-96258-022-3
Lyrik, 100 Seiten, Klappenbroschur, Englisch

*Matéi Visniec*
**MIGRAAAAANTS!** - *There's Too Many People on This Damn Boat*
ISBN: 978-3-96258-002-5
220 Pages, Theater Play, English/German

*Carmen-Francesca Banciu*
**Mother's Day** - *Song of a Sad Mother*
ISBN: 978-3-941524-47-7  *
244 Pages, English

*Jörg Rubbert*
**Paris-New York-Berlin** - *Streetphotography 1978 - 2010*
ISBN: 978-3-941524-58-3
260 Pages, Photo Retrospective, Softcover/Flaps, English/German

*Alexander de Cadenet*
**Afterbirth** - *Poems & Inversions*
ISBN: 978-3-941524-59-0
64 Pages, Poetry/Art, Softcover/Flaps, English

*Michael Lederer*
**The Great Game** - *Berlin-Warschau Express and Other Stories*
ISBN: 978-3-941524-12-5 *
242 Pages, 18 Short Stories, Softcover, English

*Carmen-Francesca Banciu*
**Berlin Is My Paris** - *Stories from the Capital*
ISBN: 978-3-941524-66-8  *
204 Pages, English

*Michael Keith*
**Perspective Drifts Like a Log on a River**
ISBN: 978-3-941524-87-3 *
200 Pages, Pensées, Softcover, English